The anthology is dedicated to my parents and siblings
for their continuous love and support

My mother, Ethel Rene Oliver (1932 – 2002)

My father, Charles Oliver

Beverly Couch

Charles Roosevelt Oliver, Jr.

Rogena Oliver (1960 – 1996)

Shelia Sanders

Lawrence Oliver

Everette Oliver

Acknowledgments/Shout Outs

There are too many members of my extended family to thank individually. Each of you provided me with so much love and attention. However I do acknowledge my neighborhood family from Hollingsworth Court. City of Little Rock Community Programs for funding various projects proposed by the *Say It Loud!* Youth Communications and Literary Arts Program. The funding made it possible for thousands of youth and community members to participate in literary events promoting reading. Director of the Central Arkansas Library System Dr. Bobby Roberts for providing much-needed office space for *Say It Loud!* and leading the charge to build state of the art libraries in neighborhoods throughout the City of Little Rock. *Say It Loud!* members and supporters past, present and future. John Cain and KABF FM 88.3 thanks for allowing young people to share their thoughts on the radio every Saturday morning. Author and educator Dr. Tony Medina provided assistance with shaping the foundation and future of Say It Loud!. Music maestro Tim Anthony you provided the pulse, the beat and the rhythm to the organization. Abiodun Oyewole your assistance with producing the CD project was most definitely one of highlights of the *Say It Loud!* program. Kenny Carroll and the crew with the DC WritersCorp the writing seminar and hospitality the organization offered to Little Rock youth in Washington, DC was very profound. jessica Care moore-Poole you provided so many opportunities for the youth. Your love and attention will never be forgotten. My cultural father Haki R. Madhubuti. I have read and reread all of your books. Now my life is committed to young people, my home filled with books and I eat whole foods most people view as unappetizing. My tenure at Third World Press proved to be one of the most defining periods in my life. Sterling Plumpp you taught me what the bop means in bebop and Blues music should be mandatory study and listening. CSPAN Book TV for giving voice to writers and literary enthusiast the opportunity to hear their voices and perspective. Tavis Smiley television and radio broadcast that encourages Black folks to think, think, think and react progressively. Black Issues Book Review the literary reviews and recommendations are always on point. Max Rodriguez and the Harlem Book Fair for the annual street festival celebrating Black literature. Black Caucus of the American Library Association for your continuing efforts to promote books and patronage of libraries. Kalama Ya Salaam and E-drum keeps us informed about numerous literary activities as well as global issues and concerns. Cliff Kelly of WVON AM 450 thanks so much for keeping Chicago well informed and reading. Michelle Smith for listening when I needed to be heard. All of the contributing writers for submitting your works. My goal was to encourage young people and community to make reading a priority. Mission accomplished because of your submissions. Literary consultant, author and publisher Jadi Keambiroiro your recommendations put me on the right track to complete this project Artist Frank Frazier the paintings you provided for the front and back covers are masterfully done and beautiful. Opal Moore I don't know what I would have done without you. Your advice, unselfishness, patience and superb editing made this project more than I imagined.

CONTENTS

Foreword   xii
Randall Horton

Introduction   xv
Patrick M. Oliver

Omar, Books and Me   1
E. Ethelbert Miller

My Nephew Erik   3
Opal Moore

Nose in a Book   6
Dr. Julianne Malveaux

Hunting Metaphors   12
Parneshia Jones

Our Lessons in Life   15
Janis F. Kearney

Books, My Nana and Me   23
Irene Smalls

Sometimes I Look Back   26
Victor Hill

For the Love of Reading   30
Marrice Coverson

(The Teachers) Whose Shoulders I Stand On   35
Dr. Sandra Y. Govan

In the Beginning There was the Word   46
Patrice Gaines

CONTENTS

Why Can't Dante Read? An Appeal to Black Parents 52
David Miller

Nerd by Nature: Proud by Choice 58
Cory Anderson

Free Public Libraries: Democracy's Real Test 63
Haki R. Madhubuti

Full Circle 70
Melrita Bonner

If You Want to Learn the Secrets of the World, Read a Book! 73
Andrew P. Jackson (Sekou Molefi Baako)

Writing and Responsibility: A Personal View 78
Dr. D.H. Melhem

Reading and Writing: The "Ever-Fixed" Compass
Towards the North Star, Freedom 81
Lynnette C. Velasco

Poem to A Young Black Mind 86
Allyson Horton

Malcolm was My Mentor 87
Jamel Shabazz

Between the Lines: Reading into the So-called "Rap Wars" 92
Dr. Ivory Achebe Toldson

Books: The Key to Our Past, Present, and Future 101
Latoya Wolfe

CONTENTS

Books are More Than Just Words   103
Traycee Lynn

Reading Make Cent$ 107
Hadassah Hickman

Telling the Stories   112
Wade Hudson

A Passion for Publishing   115
Felicia Pride

The DC WritersCorps Way   118
Kenneth Carroll

"I Want To Be A Writer," she said.   125
Opal Moore

Notes on Contributors   131

Afterword   137
Useni Eugene Perkins

FOREWORD

When *Turn the Page* originally appeared in print three years ago, the editor's goal was to show young readers, like yourself, that reading is more than a past time or a school chore—that it is empowering. The personal stories told by both established and younger writers are about how they discovered their own personal power through reading. *Turn the Page* is for young people who may not have already experienced the power of words. The writers who contributed their stories wanted to show how reading literature can be a passport to other countries or demonstrate new possibilities for the future. Their ultimate goal was to say this: you are not confined by the spaces surrounding you. You are not limited by the limitations of your neighborhood. You inhabit an entire world that is made available to you through reading. This is what these writers mean when they talk about the power of language.

Three years later, after working in literacy and reading programs across the country, I and Patrick Oliver, the editor of *Turn the Page* and creator of *Say It Loud!*, are re-sounding the literacy alarm loud and clear. The reason for this alarm is that we have seen the stunning successes of young people who didn't know what they could gain by becoming better readers and writers of the English language. For the past three years I have helped Patrick who works with young people to enhance their reading and writing skills. I have witnessed the self confidence and change that books, including *Turn the Page*, have given to our young program participants. Students who were once labeled "troubled", or "low-achievers" because of poor test scores and academic under-achievement, have blossomed because of the work we have done with *Turn the Page* and through the *Say It Loud* literacy workshops.

With that said, young people like you need to sense the urgency of this moment. In this new century you will have to take control of your destiny. This starts with knowing the fundamentals for success—reading and writing. In my line of work I meet so many teenagers who have no interest in learning or exploring through books. I recently taught a couple of creative writing workshops in a school in Washington, DC. Nearly every member of the class had trouble writing, and when I called upon them to read a passage aloud, they all declined, not because they didn't want to read, but because they could not read very well, and felt embarrassed and ashamed. Often, students try to cover their shame by acting out and being disruptive. Why I am I telling you this? I tell you this because you have seen the same behaviors in your classrooms, and maybe among your friends—how shame can lead them to act out in school, rebel at home or even drop out of school. For many this is the gateway to violence, prison, a life of missed chances. I tell you this because I am re-sounding the alarm on their behalf and yours. I have to believe books like *Turn the Page* can turn young people's lives around.

The stories and poems in this book are written by writers who have faced the same, if not harder, circumstances than some of you have faced in your short lives. If you are a young person reading this foreword, someone thought enough of you to give you this book, in hopes that it will inspire you. That person wants you to continue on a path that will help you find the education and skills you will need to make it in this society. We have now officially entered another century where reading, writing and technology are "must-have" skills if you intend to compete and succeed in the future economy. These are interesting times. The people of the United States have elected the first African American president. To understand how this country is changing we have to look at Barack Obama and how his skills as a thinker and an orator inspired the nation. More specifically, what should his life and his presidency symbolize to young people who come from broken homes and must succeed without the benefit of material wealth? Obama makes it possible for young people like you all over America and around the world to say, "Yes I Can." President Obama has been effective in gaining America's confidence because of his ability to communicate effectively and articulate ideas in a way that encompasses and embraces all Americans. With an example like President Obama, young people can see that the way to rise above inequality is to reject the role of "victim of society" or "victim of The Man" and embrace the possibilities of their own lives. Don't rationalize poor performance in school. Don't accept other people's labels. What President Obama is saying to young people and to you, through his words and the example of his life, is that you can truly be anything you want to be in this country as long as you know how to dream big. This is the message that the storytellers in *Turn the Page* want to share. This is a little book that contains a lot of big dreams. *Turn the Page* wants to help young people to dream big, bigger than what television shows you or what the latest video game will allow.

I look at the success we have had in Little Rock, Chicago and Philadelphia in helping youth become confident in reading and writing. It has been humbling. However, even with all of our successes, we understand that this work is never done, that there are still young people out there who need to be reached. That is why Patrick Oliver is re-releasing *Turn the Page*, to sound an urgent note to young people who are in danger of falling through society's cracks. Through the powerful words in this book, we want to reach into neighborhoods and difficult family situations to let you know: *Yes you can!* We want to send a message about the power of the word to change your life and the lives of others.

Be smart. Look around. See for yourself what this life is all about. History tells us that reading and writing has shown us "a way out of no way." You know it. *Now turn the page and you don't stop.*

—Randall Horton

INTRODUCTION

"**W**hy read?"
This was the question my friend and personal mentor, Dr. Amos Wilson, posed when I shared with him my interest to modify an after-school program in Little Rock, Arkansas. I had decided to build in a focus on the literary arts. He must have seen the questioning look on my face. "Why read?" he said, "That's the question you'll get from just about every one of the students you're trying to reach in your program." The question was intended to test my commitment to a program I saw as linking children and youth with books.

Dr. Wilson, a noted psychologist and author of *Awakening the Natural Genius of Black Children,* clearly understood why I wanted to modify the program. Like so many young students all over the country, a significant number of youth involved in this Little Rock program were having difficulty with reading. This reading deficiency was affecting their personal and academic lives.

With Dr. Wilson's wise counseling, I soon incorporated a literary arts program into the after school curriculum. The student-centered program now included reading sessions, creative writing, group rap sessions, CD listening, performances, parental involvement and field trips to local and national cultural events. The highlight of the new program was the opportunity for students to interact with visiting writers through in-studio radio interviews, author luncheons and author-led writing exercises. The finale of these author sessions, was a public discussion and book signing at a local college, library, community center, or church. The audience included parents, funders and sponsors.

The literary arts project not only improved students' reading ability, it opened their eyes to a larger world, making them realize that possibilities were more reachable than they had ever dreamed. They attended writing conferences and symposiums such as the Gwendolyn Brooks Writers Conference for Black Literature and Creative Writing where they met nationally recognized writers like Walter Mosley, Nikky Finney, Saul Williams, Kelly Norman Ellis, Quraysh Ali Lansana, Bakari Kitwana, Michael Dyson, and B.J. Bolden.

Toward the end of the activities, students were finally realizing that books and reading were, indeed, the window to the world. Stories expanded their horizon and their possibilities. While we did not censor what our students read, we fervently encouraged them to read thought-provoking literature that could help promote their personal growth and development. Today a number of these students have achieved college degrees and are contributing to their communities.

It is because of my first-hand experience with children and youth, watching them change before my eyes as they learned to read and grasp what they had read; it is because of the many parents and educators who articulated their desperation to find ways to help their children read, that *Turn the Page and You Don't Stop* was born. It is my hope that this anthology will give children and youth a reason to pick up that next book, or that pen and pencil. I hope that parents and teachers will use this treasure of stories and essays to instill in children and youth a love of words, stories, and books.

Many of the essays included in the anthology are reminiscent of the discussions our students had with visiting writers. In *Turn the Page and You Don't Stop* various artists, publishers and professionals discuss their love for reading and writing, and how the presence of books in their lives has contributed to their success. There is an underlying theme throughout this anthology, a passionate concern about our youth's future. Each essay offers a lesson on how literacy can play a major role in a brighter future.

Reading isn't just for "sissies," or nerds or geeks. Research shows that young people involved in after-school programs, especially reading programs, are far more likely to become productive citizens. Ask Grammy award-winning artist Erykah Badu, who participated in theater at Grambling State University; or rapper Tupac Shakur who attended the Baltimore School for the Performing Arts and wrote a book of poetry *The Rose That Grew From Concrete* (MTV Books 1999); or the NBA's Washington Wizard power forward Etan Thomas—an avid reader, high school debate team member, Syracuse University graduate and author of *More Than an Athlete* (Moore Black Press 2005). Talk to Oscar awarding-winning actor and recording artist Jamie Foxx, who was a good student and athlete at Terrell High School for the Performing Arts or another Grammy award-winner Jill Scott, who started writing poetry in middle school and recently wrote a book of poetry *The Moments, the Minutes, the Hours: The Poetry of Jill Scott* (St. Martin Press 2005).

Take the time to read *Turn the Page and You Don't Stop*. Read the stories, essays, poems and testimonials inside these pages. Don't stop there—talk about what you have read with friends, parents, brothers, sisters, cousins, classmates, teammates and church members. *Turn the Page and You Don't Stop.* The message is clear—**READ!**

—Patrick M. Oliver

OMAR, BOOKS AND ME
E. Ethelbert Miller

Folks call Omar a bookhead and me a bookend.
I don't read too much because I don't have time.
I don't even wear a watch to remind myself.

Why should I look at lines
on a page if they don't move
like the movies?

Omar reads so much about black history
and black heroes, I tell him he's gonna
be left behind living in a pyramid or something.

Omar says he looks Egyptian and maybe I should
look in the mirror and find myself too.
He laughs at me and takes a swing at my head.

*You gonna be a bookend forever with folks
pushing you out the way like you at the end
of the shelf of life.*

I listen to Omar and shake my head.
The end of the shelf of life sounds
like one of those soap shows Natalie watches.

She's always crying about some fool in love.
Omar says Natalie is my other bookend
and maybe that's why I'm afraid of books.

I laugh and tell him Natalie is his girlfriend.
You read your face Omar.
Boy, you should read your face.

I run down the street with my sneakers untied,
tripping over myself and being silly.
Omar runs after me shouting about how he plans

to bookmark my butt.
You too slow and can't run I holler
I'm running to the end of the world.

I turn the corner
as fast as Omar
can turn a page.

MY NEPHEW ERIK
Opal Moore

I can remember when a black poet was unheard of—at least in my high school they were. One day I stumbled across two poems in an anthology by writers never been mentioned by my teachers. The poems were "A Dream Deferred," by Mr. Langston Hughes, and "Children of the Poor," by Ms. Gwendolyn Brooks.

When my youngest sister told me she hated school, I gave her Langston Hughes. She never changed her mind about school but decided she loved poetry and pasted poems all over her bedroom walls, even one of her own, which was pretty good as I recall.

After Langston, she discovered Gwendolyn Brooks on her own in the poem, "We Real Cool." A very important work for my sister, because she too was *Real* cool. A fact that distressed my mother who had no other cool children.

This sister of mine now has a son, Erik, in school. "I do not hate school," Erik says. "School hates me." And one day last year Erik decided that he was sick—too sick to go to school. So he was burrowed deep into the blankets when the doorbell rang. A cute little girl, one of Erik's friends, stood in the doorway.

"Is Erik ready for school," she said. "I came to walk with him to school."

"Erik is sick," said my sister. "He's not going to school."

"Oh. That's too bad."

"You look pretty," said my sister. "What's the occasion?"

"Miss Gwendolyn Brooks is coming to our school today," she said, her voice bright with enthusiasm.

"Oh." said my sister loudly, loud enough for the sick and the dead to hear. "You say Miss Gwendolyn Brooks is going to be speaking at your school today?"

"Erik is going to miss her," said the little girl.

A few minutes later, the doorbell rang again—another little friend, in a suit and tie, looking like new money.

"Is Erik gone yet?"

"Erik is sick."

"He's gonna miss Miss Gwendolyn Brooks," said the boy.

"I know," said my sister.

By the time the doorbell rang a third time, Erik was up, washed, pressed, and on his way to see Miss Gwendolyn Brooks who was speaking at his school that day. "I think I feel much better," he said, as the door slammed behind him.

Many claims have been made for the power of poetry to free our minds, inspire the disheartened, provide the language of love. Poet Gwendolyn Brooks, being more modest, said simply that poetry was Life, Distilled.

But I remember when poetry could heal the sick and raise my nephew Erik.

Jamel Shabazz

Nose In A Book
Dr. Julianne Malveaux

"**Y**ou have always got your nose in a book," my mother yelled at me. As my siblings swirled around me doing chores, I read. A moody 13, I was more enthralled by the printed word than anything that was happening in my own life. I used to take the *World Book Encyclopedia* and line it up on our hallway floor, so that when, at the end of an entry, they directed you to see something else, I'd already have it ready for an uninterrupted read. I had read my way around the African continent nearly a decade before my toes hit African soil, and while the encyclopedic entries gave me just a scant idea of what to expect, there was something rich and sweet about the process of expecting. And so, I knew New York before I got there, thought I understood the Harlem Renaissance before I'd laid eyes on the Schomburg Center for Research in Black Culture. I had "gone south" before getting there, inhaled the legislative process before coming to Washington, and had even fallen in and out of love with a brother who came to life through the printed world.

Maybe I take it just a bit to the extreme, but reading is one of life's very special pleasures. Through the printed word, whole worlds can come to life, feelings can be transmitted, passions for social justice enflamed. All you have to do is read Martin Luther King's *Why We Can't Wait,* or W.E.B. DuBois' *Souls of Black Folk* to understand the challenges that African American people have always faced. Check out Maya Angelou's *I Know Why the Caged Bird Sings* to get a sense of coming of age (or, for that matter, read her latest cookbook to understand the symbiotic connection between feelings and feeding). If you ever think you are "losing it", Sylvia Path's *The Bell Jar* puts all of that in perspective. The matter of romantic compromise is deftly handled in Toni Cade Bambara's short story "The Johnson Girls" from the short story collection, *Gorilla, My Love*.

Before *Beloved* became a movie, Toni Morrison brought the beauty shop to life, down to the smell of fresh-fried hair and the tang of Dixie Peach in her book, *The Bluest Eye*. Her tale of female friendship, in *Sula* reveals a secret sisterhood that many of us have experienced. Our poets, too, evoke, provoke and bring on the smiles. Where have you gone, wrote Mari Evans, with your confident walk your crooked smile? Can't you see the loping swagger? My heart in one pocket, she writes, rent money in the other. Don't you know the roguish charmer, the brother who talked you out of your last five cents, the one you might have paid for the performance if you, too, were not at the end of your rope. That's good writing, evocative, and memorable, the stuff that makes you want to keep your nose in a book.

I am a fairly indiscriminate reader. I love reading both fiction and nonfiction by African American authors, but I have been accused of reading soup cans when I'm bored. I love to read history—both in fictional form and straight, with no chaser. When I read, I talk back. And in order to talk back, I sometimes have to tackle those dead white males that did black folks so wrong with their equivocating about issues like slavery. When I read David McCullough's biography of John Adams, I appreciated Adams for the attention he gave his wife, Abigail, but also was utterly furious that he knew he was wrong on the slavery issue, but was content to be wrong. He said that future generations would have to deal with issues of race, and acknowledged that he sacrificed black folks to save the union. It still makes me want to holler.

Turn The Page and You Don't Stop!

The progressive historian Howard Zinn writes about the histories we learn and those we do not. We know about President John Adams, but not about the slaves who cooked his breakfast, and those who cleaned his house. We know the famous Frederick Douglass story because he was educated enough to write it, but we only see his wife, Anna Murray, the woman who helped him escape but then sat at the sidelines of his success, through the eyes of others. Jewell Parker Rhodes (in her book *Douglass's Women: A Novel*) wrote of her in historical fiction, but imagine that we had her biography, in her own words.

History is written, they say, by the winners. From that perspective, it makes sense that we elevate white men in leadership positions and ignore those black folks, women and other people of color whose contribution, though significant, is hidden because they weren't perceived as winners. When I read the stories from the perspective of the so-called victors, I am always wondering what the silent would say. We know that a brother made it to the North Pole before the so-called discoverer did! Did Shakespeare's sisters write his plays? Why won't August Wilson get the same play? Do James Baldwin, Paule Marshall and Nikki Giovanni belong in the "canon" of central literature because their stuff is as good as Herman Melville's, Edgar Allen Poe's and Ernest Hemingway's. For that matter, why are folks so agitated about the bad girl and bad boy behavior of the 21st century when many of the writers of a century ago absolutely enjoyed acting out? Come on —Hemingway courted death and eventually killed himself. Mary McCarthy was belligerently angry with many of her peers, and worked all of that drama out in public. The Algonquin room was yesterday's equivalent of today's downtown club. Back then, talented writers and their bad behavior earned a wink and a nod from reviewers because of their talent and because of an old boy/girl network. Fast forward. Think about it.

I don't do much science fiction, because I think that being black in white America is too much like living science fiction, especially with the insanity and the stereotypes that shape our existence. I'm reacting, of course, to the bizarre confidence with which a former Secretary of Education would propose a "thought experiment" like aborting all of our nation's black babies. Of course, good science fiction would give me the imaginatory tools to abort his mouth, to, perhaps, place a trap on it, or to allow one of his incisors to grow sharp when he uttered ignorant and racist crap.

The kumbaya crowd will tell me that there has been a misunder-standing, that the Secretary didn't mean what he said and that he is not a racist. I say that I know what I heard and I condemn him, in the harshest terms, for it. We simply do not speak the same language or have the same sensibilities. Yet there are science fiction writers, phenomenal African American women, who write eloquently of cultural misunderstanding through science fiction. I love Octavia Butler's work (especially *Kindred*, and *The Parable of The Sower*) and also Tananarive Due's (notably *The Good House* and *The Living Blood*). They bring the strange to life in a contemporary context, and stimulate my imagination.

In my own field of economics, there is a rich and fascinating body of knowledge that has emerged absent the African American perspective. John Kenneth Galbraith, the wonderful and progressive economist, managed to mention us only in passing, but we make our appearance in Gunnar Myrdal's *The American Dilemma*, and also in

TURN THE PAGE AND YOU DON'T STOP!

Oliver Cromwell *Cox's Caste, Class,* and *Race* (Elliot Liebow's *Talley's Corner* is an ethnographic study that now reads like fatally focused fiction. Missing in economic writing are biographies of those early economists, especially of the women like Dr. Sadie Tanner Mosell Alexander (1898-1989) and Dr. Phyllis Ann Wallace (1921-1993). We need to know about their work, but also about their intellectual development and about the texture of their lives.

I so love the printed word that I'd love you, the readers of this essay, to share that love. To love the notion that print can make other worlds come alive for us. To love the fact that we can communicate thoughts and ideas to each other through print. To literally be tickled by words and that which they convey. To be transported out of a static present space and into an electric future, just through print.

Print has taken me through hard times. Three years ago, a bad mammogram introduced the possibility of breast cancer into my life. My friends laughed that the first place I went was to the Internet, to find a book, *A Year To Live* (by Stephen Levine) to reassure me. Yes, it was a little morbid, but the printed word said more to me than a counselor or friend could. I needed the love and support of my friends, but I also needed the printed reminder that others had gone through this, that everything would be okay.

Here is my mantra—when in doubt, read. Read when you are happy, read when you are sad. Read when you are lonely. Read when you are mad. Read when you need guidance, and when you need to smile. Read when you need to escape, even for a little while.

You have always got your nose in a book, my mama says to me now. As an adult, I can still think of no greater pleasure than sitting in her home, looking through her library, and grabbing something to read. *The apple doesn't fall far from the tree; there is not a single room in her home where you won't find a book; in amazing symmetry, the same is true of my home, from the basement to the bathroom.* Yes, I always have my nose in a book, because books are my bridge to the world.

HUNTING METAPHORS
Parneshia Jones

❂ **Afternoons** ❂

Daylight watches me
sitting at my girlhood desk
I was never able to part from.

White blue-lined paper thirsty
for metaphors pooling in my head.
Black Warrior pencils engrave
my thoughts in bound journals
given as gifts or bought at rummage sales.

The dictionary and Synonym Finder,
my two writing bibles, have permanent
places among endless sheets of revisions.

A laptop has replaced the typewriter
pictures of my grandmother and postcards
taped to the wall and an old broken
wind chime that stopped singing long ago,
hangs from a nail in the wall

Poetry books, philosophical thought,
memoirs and novels line four walls
creating a rainbow of bindings.

Hughes and Walker, Ellis and Wilkinson,
Brooks, Neruda, Socrates and Lee.
Their words wrapped in book lockets
lined up like soldiers on my shelves,
watching me like guardian angels of literature.

Dusk approaches the horizon like a first kiss,
my words dim down to the night, but my
pencil keeps moving through the changing sky...

*   Nights   *
The peek hours of metaphors,
words come out like hunters stitching
native patterns on quilt like paper.

I am hungry for the verse.
My predatory eyes hunt the Thesaurus,
feeding on new words by the hour.
Stanzas shaping themselves on the page,
fingers almost numb to the pencil's pressure.

TURN THE PAGE AND YOU DON'T STOP!

The night paces behind me.
The rest of the world sleeps.
Silence has never sounded so loud.

Delicate sheets of college ruled paper
torn and crumbled in the hunt,
lying on the floor like victims.
Broken pencils that gave up in the fight,
replaced with blue ink marking its territory.

I am eager, starving for that last image
the final endings not willing to leave,
until the good fight had been fought to the end.

The pen dries itself to exhaustion,
the pages surrender to a thousand words
and I leave the desk full and satisfied.
The hunt is over and I lie my spear down
leaving a desk full of poems to embrace the sunrise...

❋ **Mornings** ❋
The desk lies in state.
I was never one to write in the mornings.
My pencils and journals are relieved.

OUR LESSONS IN LIFE
Janis F. Kearney

I was four years old when daddy introduced me to the magical world of learning. Like my siblings before me, I was introduced to education at James Kearney's knee. This raggedly handsome pied piper spent hours bent over a book, lulling me into learning as I breathed in the sharp fragrance of his Pall Mall cigarette, and watched it bleed ashes onto the dark wood porch slats. His deep, gravelly voice mesmerized, making his words that much more important. His pause, as he took a deep draw from the dwindling cigarette, invited my childish questions.

James Kearney had his own ways and theories about teaching his children. He was convinced that his own love for learning could be transferred to his children. One by one, he taught us the rudiments of counting, identifying our alphabets, our colors and how to pronounce the simplest of words. "C-A-T, spells what? Come on, you remember... it sounds like hat." He responded to our correct answers with giant smiles, as if we'd performed a Shakespearean soliloquy. As the evening turned a reddish hue of grey, and the cricket chirps became a part of the dusk, daddy begrudgingly closed the book, or folded the one sheet of paper in half. He stood, patting me on the head before going inside. "Okay...that was a good lesson. Tomorrow, we'll learn some more."

There was never an ounce of rancor in his laughter when I made childish mistakes. His mild caution, was, "You got to remember to always do your very best." And, because I'd hear this throughout the years I lived on Varner Road, I knew it was something he believed was important. In later years, my mistakes would garner sterner admonishments. "You gotta work hard, now, Faye. Getting' it almost right, or coming up second don't mean a hill of beans in this world." Lucky, visionary or both, daddy caught his children just as our minds and hearts became ripe for the picking. And, it was during those early years that he transferred all his love for learning and the written words, into our hearts and minds. And, it stuck.

James Kearney was a study in contrasts when it came to his cotton crops and our education. We were raised to take his ravenous love for learning, and determination to raise children who used their brains, as a given. We also realized that he was just as determined not to raise a bunch of "good for nothing children," who didn't know the value of hard work. This was the part of daddy that justified him to putting his crops before his children's education during the first quarters of school. While our minds depended on all the things he taught us as toddlers; our—and, his—day to day existence, depended on this latter determination. James and Ethel Kearney's infrequent arguments were centered on this conflict between school and work.

"Children got to learn the importance of work or they grow up to be useless," daddy fussed back, when mama begged him to send their children to school. In daddy's mind, his children helping with the cotton crop was just plain common sense, and the only way the Kearney family could survive. "James, don't it matter to you that this gone put our children behind the others in school? They already make fun of us, and call our children church mice." It was more than that tearing at mama's heart. Her bitter memories of the education that eluded her as a child, was still fresh in her mind.

She wouldn't let up. Her children's education was more important than anything she could think of—and, just as important as their embracing Christianity. "James, I'm already helping you in the fields all day. The children can help out after they come from school...I just don't want none of them to fall behind in their classes. I'm scared they may not be able to catch back up."

While Ethel Curry Kearney was never one to ask for favors for herself, she didn't blink an eye about asking for her children. We were the only thing in her life that brought out that side of her she kept hid from the world—her soft emotions that she always feared others would see as a weakness. Daddy hated more than anything to see his wife's sadness, and because of that he promised to see to it that none of his children fell behind in school. "Ain't none of these children gone fall behind, Ethel. You'll see."

Most of us never experienced attending school during the fall season—September, October or November. We spent the first three months of the fall semester helping daddy get his cotton bales out before the weather turned. Other children might have loved such freedom from the drudgery of books and the structure of a classroom. The Kearney children craved what they were missing. We spent our nights talking about school, and books and the intricacies of being a real student.

James Kearney made good on his promise. Rarely did a Kearney child fall far behind in our classes, and if we did, we always caught back up once we resumed regular attendance. And, though we weren't on the normal education schedule, schooling began at our home the same day it did for the rest of Gould's children. We were allowed to attend school the first week or so, before cotton picking season had fully begun. We were filled with excitement and anticipation as we rode the long, yellow school bus with the other children living up and down Varner Road.

During those wonderful days, we would gather our books and the instructors' guidance sheets the teachers gave out at the beginning of each school year. The books and guide sheets were our maps for the rest of the semester, whether we were sitting in the school classroom or not.

Our education was a family affair. During fall evenings, after we'd eaten mama's dinner and cleared the table of dishes; we gathered there for our daily study sessions. My father's attentiveness to us, I learned later in life, had a lot to do with the loss of his own father when he was just nine years old. He had left his home and his mother at the very early age of 11 years old, to find his own way in the world. Much of our awe of our father had to do with the numerous tales of his travel and the people he'd met during his vagabond-like childhood.

Though most of our fall days were centered around daddy's 50 acres of rented cotton fields that subsidized our food and clothing for the rest of the year, our nights were dedicated to feeding our minds. My father's clear vision that these daily exercises were investments in his children's futures was a great deal loftier than ours. We saw these evenings simply as wonderful respites from the harsh realities of our everyday existence.

In spite of everything, our home was always filled with laughter. Now, I know it was a kind of balm to soothe the parts of our existence we refused to look at. We had strong, hearty laughs that came from somewhere deep in our cores. Both our parents joined in, at times, with our humor; though my mother tried hard to hold on to a certain décor in her laughter. Often times, we laughed derisively at each other, in spite of our parents' promised punishments for "picking on" one or the other of our siblings. The only thing that ever tempered our laughter was the guarantee that our time would come.

Though daddy had gone no further than the 10th grade, he told us, proudly, that he never stopped learning. "Anywhere I ended up, I found me a library, or somewhere that had books I could borrow." My parents each had good reasons to make sure they didn't raise a houseful of illiterate children. Besides the regrets that they had missed out on a completed education, they were convinced that education was their children's key out of the poverty that restricted their own freedom.

To James and Ethel Kearney's credit, and to blessings from on high, we took to learning like tadpoles to muddy bayou water. It seemed that each successive child learned earlier than the one before. We scoured daddy's well-worn bibles, milk cartons, oatmeal boxes, the few precious books in the house, the four-page *Lincoln Ledger* newspaper daddy picked up in Star City; the monthly cooperative extension magazine mama received as a member, and her coveted recipe books she used on special occasions. Nothing was safe from our hungry eyes and minds.

We settled down to our nightly homework sessions shortly after dinner—the only time the Kearney household experienced complete quiet, except when we slept. The only sounds in the house at those times was the scraping of our pencils on the thin, lined sheets of paper; quiet mumbling as we read the night's lessons to ourselves, or some child asking daddy a question about something he might know the answer to. One of our parents was always there. In our early years, there presence was a necessity, later, it was more comforting habit for us and our parents, than necessity.

Jo Ann was usually sitting next to daddy quietly explaining her lessons to him, rather than the other way around. At the earliest age, she was a child whose brilliance demanded our respect. In many ways, Jo Ann was Daddy's model child. He lavished praise on her, not only because he was proud of her, but because of her dark beauty, he was bent on proving to the world that the color of her skin had nothing to do with her intelligence.

The sibling rivalry between my sister and I began during those early years, when I slowly became resentful and jealous of my 18-month younger sister. Because of my father's "modeling" her before us, Jo Ann's consistency in bringing home A's and A-plus', while I brought home a mixture of A's, B's, and sometimes, a smattering of C's. My resentment was daunted, only by Jo Ann's generosity with our younger siblings who often asked her to help with their homework.

Mama rarely sat all the way through our evening lessons. Her self-imposed curfew was 8 p.m., early enough to get a good night's sleep, and still be ready for her day when she awoke at four, the next morning. "Alright, I'm gone to bed, now. Y'all need to finish up before long, and get ready for bed. Make sure they don't stay up too late, James...it's hard enough to get the boys up in the morning." She said one hearty "Goodnight," to all of us, and made her way down the hallway. Most nights, she'd remind Jo Ann and me of our nightly chore. "Faye and Jo Ann, don't forget those dishes before you go to bed. I don't want to have to look no dirty dishes when I get up in the morning."

Jo Ann had a vitriol dislike for washing dishes. To my continued dismay, when I refused to cave in and wash dishes when it was Jo Ann's night; we were both awakened the next morning by mama's voice, and the feel of her wielding either a skinny switch or a thick belt. "A hard head makes a soft behind!" she said, more times than I can remember, as she lashed at our legs through the cover, then directly on our bare legs to make sure we got the message.

Yet, even mama's painful wake-up calls didn't change Jo Ann's mind about this evening chore relegated to the two of us. "It's not fair," she'd say, her pretty face twisted in frowns. "Why we got to wash dishes...why those stupid boys get to go outside and swim in the bayou while we wash dishes and clean the house?" In my parent's provincial household, boys did outside work and girls did inside house work. While we never had to get up in the middle of the night and find the cows or hogs that had found their way out of their pens, we also couldn't join the boys in leisurely swims, winter skating on the frozen water, or go hunting in the woods.

That delegation of roles never changed, no matter how much Jo Ann fussed about it. And, because Jo Ann decided she'd rebel against my parents' traditions by refusing to carry her part of the load, I was destined to wash twice as many dishes in the Kearney household, than I would have, had she been a more malleable sister. That, or we would continue to be awakened by mama's switch, and admonitions about our "hard heads and soft behinds."

Our parents had been intricately involved in our education for all the 30-odd years their 17 children attended schools. They had served many of those years on the PTA Board. The fact that they knew most people whispered about them behind their backs, didn't keep them from getting involved at the schools, and being vocal about things they felt strongly about. The couple, in fact, encouraged a kind of awe from the other parents upon their discovery that they weren't just poor, colored sharecroppers with a house full of children. There was something different about this good-looking, proud couple who were bent on seeing theirs and other children got an adequate education from Gould's schools.

"Mama, I got all A's!" That could have been any one of my siblings on report card day, proudly offering proof of their good work for my parents' approval. This was a special day, something we almost always looked forward to. "That's my girl!" daddy would exclaim with a broad smile on his face. Nothing meant as much to us as making our parents proud. There was something almost ceremonial in our march off the long, yellow bus, into our home on Varner road on that day. A raggedy line formed, as each of us presented documented proof of our superior class performance over the last nine weeks. The fact that we might have missed half of the days during that nine weeks, was no excuse for falling short of excellence in our parent's minds. My parents demanded our best—and, our report cards were documentation of that.

The times I fell short of living up to my parents' expectations, and brought home less than stellar grades, are still etched deep in my memory. "Girl, what have you been doing all these nine weeks?" mama would ask, the hurt showing in her eyes. I would hang my head, never offering the answers I already knew would forfeit the first smack, or commands to "go and get me a switch." Without their saying it, I always knew when I'd let my parents down. The pain from the whippings never lasted as long as my disappointment in myself.

Books, My Nana and Me
Irene Smalls

Story is how I found myself. In stories, I found out I was lost, but in story I also found out I didn't have to stay lost. I could find my way. The life and family that nature had placed me in was not a good fit. Books gave me the power to change my circumstances. It was mix and match. I took a swatch from Paul Lawrence Dunbar's *Lil Brown Baby with the Sparkling Eyes,* a cup from *A Tree Grows in Brooklyn* by Betty Smith, pieces of *No Images* by Waring Cuney, a whole chapter from *Women who Run with the Wolves* by Clarissa Pinkola Estes and a dab from *Passages* by Gail Sheehy, just to name a few. In books, in stories, I was able to discover who I was, how I was and, most importantly, how to make a life not based on just what was immediately around me. I realized I could make my own organically derived formula for making a life. I understood that this derivative life I envisioned and implement was based on the global community and thousands of years of human history. I could learn from their success and mistakes. Being born poor, female and black is no excuse in a society that forgives none of the above but your life is what you make it. Money talks, excuses and BS take a long walk to nowhere. When life gives you lemons, don't just make lemonade. Read a book on how to merchandise, market and distribute your lemonade. Develop a secret formula, copyright it, and franchise your lemonade. The world has many lemonade stands but too few lemonade moguls.

Books were especially important for me because no one read to me or told me stories. The adults in my life, both the good ones and the ill-intentioned, were busy trying to figure things out for their lives.

TURN THE PAGE AND YOU DON'T STOP!

Often I was in the way, but with a book in my hand I was the perfect child. "Children should be seen and not heard" was the fifties adage.

I grew up in a family where my caretaker, my Nana, had only finished second grade. She didn't know how to read. But her illiteracy was a fire under her belly. She made sure I read, went to the library, and did my homework. And, you know something, I got to like it. For her, illiteracy was a curse, something she was heaven bound to make sure I did not suffer. So, being a thinking being, I found out early that whenever I had chores to do, or something I didn't particularly want to do, all I had to do was to open a book and instantly the dishes, the dusting were subordinated to my reading. Boy, I read a lot. But, while I was reading (OK I'm being honest) and shirking my duties, there was a beatiful smile on my Nana's face as she dusted or washed the dishes in my stead. Well, there was a whole lot of housework to do in my Nana's house the motto was "Cleanliness is next to Godliness." My Nana made sure she was bound for heaven's glory with the window washing, daily floor washing with bleach and dusting, every day laundry, etc. In my "neatnik" Nana's house even with me taking the maximum number of books out of the library every Saturday by midweek I had read all my books. I was in crisis. It was time for drastic measures. I decided to memorize the dictionary during those awkward moments when the possibility of my having to do some housework loomed its ugly head. In memorizing the unabridged dictionary I had ample reading stuff to keep my Nana smiling and my hands out of dishwater. Feeling just a tad selfish in my quest of laziness, I started to read out loud the stories and the poems. Sometimes, she would interrupt and ask for the definition of a word from the book. My dictionary skills were secure. I would recite it from memory or, if I hadn't gotten to that letter of the alphabet yet, I would look it up. Carefully reading the word, the correct pronunciations, whether it was a noun, pronoun or adjective or other part of speech, the derivations of the word and finally, all of the definitions. And when I pronounced the dictionary's words I had to use the most proper English. I would speak in a loud sonorous voice, the beginnings of my public speaking career. "Don't say ain't," my Nana always told me, "cause people judge you on how you speak." Then, we would go back to the book and resume our story of travel, adventure, love, or adolescence. Magically, I taught her to read.

All that I am I owe to those times, to Nana and her special way of imbuing me with a love of books and all things reading. Because books and reading were almost reverential to her they became vital to me and to my life. Also I got a near perfect score on the verbal part of the Scholastic Aptitude Test several years later, which lead to a full college scholarship at Cornell University, an Ivy League school. Sometimes I wonder who tricked whom. My latest multi-cultural picture book is *My Nana and Me* published by Little Brown and Company dedicated to my wonderful Nana. I even put a picture of my Nana in the front of the book so everyone could see how beautiful she was. Thank you Nana.

Sometimes I Look Back
Victor Hill

I was a "country boy." I have no idea when I came to see myself as such, but I don't recall ever regarding myself any other way I was raised in a rural community that sat eight to ten miles south of Little Rock in central Arkansas. Eight to ten miles doesn't seem like a long way now, but back in the late 1950s and early 1960s, it seemed like a considerable distance. Woods surrounded my family's house. Many people in the community grew gardens and kept hog pens. On occasion we would make the trip from what we called "the county" to "town." Everybody knew everybody and there was a sense of belonging and mutual responsibility, which is what I mean by community. I think those things are inherent in the term.

My father was and is a natural farmer. He has a closeness to the land and to nature that I hope I have inherited, if only in the smallest quantity. He always talked of self-sufficiency and learning to "live off the land." To this day, I live as simple and natural a life style as possible. I pick, wash and put up greens and peas from my father's garden and have planned out my own.

My mother was and is a born teacher. Most people who know my family agree that I particularly take after my mother in personality and temperament. She loves learning and imparting knowledge to others. She was also in some sense a scientist, and her children were among her earliest guinea pigs. She taught us to read at a very early age. In fact, I have no recollection of not knowing how to read. I recall at the age of four writing and illustrating stories for my own amusement as I waited for my older brother to return home from school. I have always loved being around books, paper, pencils and pens. I still do to this day. I have owned two homes in the last fifteen years. In each one I had a library built in one of the rooms. I can hardly imagine living in a house without a library and a gym in it. What would be the point?

Like most children, I wanted to be as much like everyone else as I could. But I had several qualities that marked me as different, the most notable of which was my eye condition. I have a condition called "convergent strabismus." My right eye turns inward noticeably giving me the appearance of being "cross-eyed." Such being the case, I was the butt of a great many jokes, a great amount of teasing, and maybe worst of all, pejorative assumptions about my intellectual capabilities. It was always a social handicap; when I was thirty and had graduated from law school, I learned that it was considered a physical handicap. To me, it was a huge inconvenience, and often an embarrassment. I still have a habit of looking down or away when I speak to people. Just the same, despite the opinions of the experts, I never regarded myself as being physically handicapped. Compared to truly handicapped people, my condition is nothing more than a minor annoyance.

When I was in elementary school, the schools had not yet become desegregated. We were separate but far from equal in the facilities and equipment at our disposal. The teachers, however, were first-rate. This was so, I think, because they cared about the children on a personal level. They had a first-hand understanding of the challenges that we would face and they were determined to prepare us to meet them to the best of their ability. There was one teacher who would exhort us on a regular basis to, "Read, colored people, read!" She said it with great urgency.

TURN THE PAGE AND YOU DON'T STOP!

I did read, and needed no prompting. In those days, something called the Bookmobile would make regular rounds down in "the country." It was like a mini-library on wheels. It would stop at a certain location for a while to allow the children to browse and make selections from the shelves. A week or two later, it would return to retrieve the books and allow other selections to be made. I loved the Bookmobile.

From time to time, my mother would take us to the public library in Little Rock. I would never know where to start. I wanted to touch and smell and read every book in the building. Being surrounded by books was about the closest thing to Heaven I could imagine. For some reason, I developed a fascination for martial arts and mythology. I eventually read every book I could get my hands on in both categories. I seem to recall regarding mythology as being like comic books without the pictures. I would supply the pictures either by drawing them or by simply fashioning them in my imagination.

It was during these trips to the library that I decided that I wanted to earn a black belt in some martial art and a master's degree in either philosophy or engineering. I met some remarkable teachers and accomplished both those goals while still in my early twenties.

I went on to go to law school and worked as a legal aid lawyer for about fourteen years. I was prevailed upon to run for circuit judge to replace the sole African-American circuit judge in this district, who had decided to retire. Being introverted and reclusive all my life, I initially resisted. Eventually, I agreed to run for the position and won the election. I am now in my sixth year on the bench. I am still "cross-eyed," still introverted and reclusive. I still love to read everything in sight. With all the briefs, cases and other items that I have to read daily, that comes in handy.

I have learned a number of lessons over the years. Most of them are lessons taught to me by the challenges that I faced in life. They are:

1. Don't go around feeling sorry for yourself. Look around; somebody's worse off than you are.

2. Prepare yourself. Train physically as if you had a world title fight coming up; you never can tell. Study constantly. Hone your mind as if all humanity was relying on you to do great things; because it is. Look to your soul. Monitor your thoughts, words, motives and deeds as if a benevolent and omniscient God were watching your every thought; I believe this to be so.

3. When it comes to personal accomplishment, it's good to have people around you who believe in you, but ultimately what you think of yourself far out-weighs what anyone else thinks of you.

4. Never accept less than the absolute best that you have to offer at whatever you do. Remember that mastery and mediocrity are both habits. The one that will prevail is the one that you decide to culti-vate.

5. Take your duties and responsibilities seriously but don't take yourself all that seriously. Laugh at your-self sometimes, everybody else probably is. You might as well join in the fun.

6. Whatever you do, be guided by principle, and foremost among these should be honor and personal integrity.

29

FOR THE LOVE OF READING
Marrice Coverson

My memories of Sumner, Mississippi, are always closely followed by memories of my grandma. Those memories are tinged with both nostalgia and sadness. Nostalgia, because she played such an important role in my early childhood, and sadness, because so many of the lessons she taught me, I failed to put into practice until it was too late to say "Thank you." In fact, like most young people, I didn't value those teachings until much too late.

I know now that grandma did the best she could. The things she didn't give me had more to do with what was passed on to her, than with her love for me. No one had told her that reading and books have the power to transform us from who we are, to who we want to be. But, they say God watches over children and fools, and he must have decided to instill that very deep love for reading and for learning inside me...in spite of the fact that grandmother never understood that love.

Grandma, like so many black southern parents, took her parenting responsibility very seriously, but that responsibility didn't include expressing love or the softer side of her emotions to us. She was convinced that energy was better utilized instilling in us lessons we'd need to "make it in the world." Those teachings included hard work, religious faith and morality; they offered very little about the power of education and reading. She taught what she knew, and what her mother or grandmother had passed on to her.

In my own mind, my migration from Mississippi to Chicago in 1971, was about making a better life for myself. Much later, and after much soul-searching, I would discover that leaving Mississippi and grandma was also about leaving my past behind, distancing myself from my harsh realities of growing up in a poor, hopeless environment, and from many of the teachings grandma had instilled in me.

Funny, how our pasts seem to always find a way of catching up with us, even if we are lucky enough to make a better life for ourselves. It was 1998 when mine found me and made me realize that my future was inextricably tied to my experiences in Sumner, Mississippi. It was that day that I learned to value ALL of my experiences, the good and the bad; because they each have their own lessons.

I was on my way back to Mississippi that day. It was far from my first trip back, but it would prove to be one of the most important. I slept part of the way, and must have been half-dreaming as I saw that tiny little girl who had once been me...I still hated the word, but the pain wasn't as sharp as it had been 25 years earlier. Grandma and I had done pretty well, I thought; as well as could be expected, as the old folks used to say.

I remembered the times grandma had caught me hiding with a book, and how she'd admonished me that I was wasting precious time that should be spent working. In grandma's world, domestic work was honest work; and, sadly, her own limited expectations prevented her from seeing anything beyond that for me—to finish high school, secure a job with one of the wealthy white women in the neighborhood, or begin a life of manual labor in the wealthy white farmers' cotton fields.

I, of course, wanted something different, something more, and I believed my love for reading would be the pathway to that different life. We had very few books in our home, but I savored the few we did have. More than anything else, I loved to read and dream about my own life mirroring that of the girls and boys I read about in those books. We didn't have a television, and now I know that was a blessing in disguise. I was forced to use my imagination, rather than to be force-fed other people's fantasies.

Neighbors who worked for wealthy white families brought me magazines: *Good Housekeeping, The Saturday Evening Post, Life.* I would be less than honest if I didn't admit that *True Romance* was my favorite. To grandma's great satisfaction, I also read the Bible as avidly as I read the rest, and I was proud to announce to her that I'd read it from cover to cover—more than once! Reading transformed me like nothing else could.

Schools were an extension of books for me. I enjoyed going to our small, all-black schools. Even knowing our books had been sent from the white schools, they were still valuable. My teachers, most of whom were neighbors, encouraged me in school. The high school principal and his wife urged me to continue my education after graduating. "You can do it," they'd tell me. "You can go to college."

Whether it was their encouragement, or simply my need to move beyond what I knew, I applied to college, and with the help of social security assistance and a work-study job, I was able to enter college. I graduated with a B.A. in Sociology. My first job was with the Home Reading Program at Beacon House in Chicago. My job was to work with parents of preschool children, training and encouraging them to participate in their children's early learning experiences by reading to them.

During my years in Chicago, I held a number of jobs in the non-profit world, and always felt satisfied with the direction of my career …until that fateful airplane ride from Chicago to Mississippi. Whether a secret message was written in those white, billowing clouds, or a small voice whispered to me from afar, I realized during that flight that my past would soon become a part of my future.

I knew my life would now be centered around empowering young children, especially African American children, through books and reading. I would be tasked with transferring my own love for words to youth who hadn't yet learned that power.

I had made a stab at helping "fix" some of the problems youth encountered during earlier jobs. Children had always been important to me. I had always believed I could empathize with their frailties and their fears. But, instead of becoming a lead administrator in someone else's program, I was to start and lead one of my own. I knew it would be a leap of faith, but we never know just how much of a leap we're taking until we actually get into the middle of it! I rolled up my sleeves, and began the process that led to the development of the Open Book Program.

It's not only fear of hard work, but a fear of failure that prevents so many of us from reaching for our dreams. It's scary knowing you're attempting to build something from scratch, and that the success or failure of that something is on your shoulders. I was giving up a known, my executive director's position, for an unknown, a reading program that I wasn't sure the education and parental communities would even accept.

But some things are simply meant to be, and I'm convinced that the Open Book Program was one of those things. Somehow, everything suddenly fell into place. Loyola University accepted my proposal and Mayo Elementary School agreed to host the pilot. The right people appeared. The right connections were made. We were on our way!

TURN THE PAGE AND YOU DON'T STOP!

The pilot for the Open Book Program took place in spring 1999 at Mayo Elementary School. Twenty-five excited young people participated in the after school program. My vision was taking shape before my eyes. We chose *Dance Kayla!* by Chicago author Darwin McBeth Walton, as our pilot book. It brought tears to my eyes to see the children entranced by this black author's book about a young black girl who sought her destiny as a dancer.

In 2005, the Open Book program celebrated seven years of existence, and growth—from that one small pilot site, to eight school sites. In my heart, I celebrate the fact that black youth in inner-city Chicago are reading and discussing the work of black authors—Sandra Belton, Ashley Bryan, Debbi Chocolate, Sharon Draper, Sharon F. Flake, Jan Spivey Gilchrist, Nikki Grimes, Walter Dean Myers, Harriette Gillem Robinet, Charles R. Smith, Jr., Glennette Tilley Turner, and Camille Yarbrough—experiences I never had growing up in Mississippi.

So much has happened since that little girl down in the Mississippi Delta hid from her grandma to read, since that airplane ride that set this second phase of my life in action. I am grateful for this one lesson: that it is often things we want for ourselves that inform who we become, and what we give to others. Reading and books are certainly such things for me.

THE TEACHERS
(ON WHOSE SHOULDERS I STAND)
Sandra Y. Govan

Although they frequently functioned as petty deities within the tightly structured cosmologies they created, those teachers who instructed us in the olden "golden days" of the 1950s were not gods, thus not wholly infallible. If, however, you valued your life, you certainly could not have told them that, nor informed your parents that your teachers were wrong, nor even voiced so perilous a thought aloud. In those days teachers ruled with tremendous power, a power they directed toward the children in their charge in whatever manner they chose. They could hurt or heal; they could snatch you down from a cloud or worse, they could pluck you out from among your peers and stand you on a pedestal above your peers as the model child, insist other, lesser, children should look up to you, gravitate toward you, emulate you–thus making you a ripe target.

Some teachers used their power wisely. Like the tall, thin, soft-spoken, elegant and regal Miss Auld, my fourth grade teacher, they were kindly, gentle, compassionate. It was Miss Auld, I recall, who sat down at her desk to explain, after overhearing me whine, "I'm tired of always being the smallest and always having to stand in the front of the line," that everyone had problems. "Because I'm so tall," she confided one afternoon while seated at her desk, "people are always asking me to take something down from a cabinet that they cannot reach. Or," she continued, "they tease me by constantly asking annoying questions. 'How's the weather up there?' they'll say and think they're funny. It can be very aggravating sometimes to be a tall girl. You should be glad you're so pretty and petite. Stand at the head of that line with pride."

Others, like my tyrannical third grade teacher, Miss Vigor, or the severe seventh grade teacher, Mr. Murkey, were spiteful, hostile, even malevolent. Still, the vast majority of teachers I encountered in those precious years between kindergarten and eighth grade endeavored to be caring, encouraging and supportive; they challenged you to learn by any means necessary. And, most of them, despite their sometimes "unorthodox" methods, clearly cared about the whole child, not just the test scores the child earned.

Because I went through primary school in Chicago in the fifties and early sixties, and because I came into the world with dislocated hips, an impairment that forced my parents to place me in several of the public specialized schools servicing handicapped children before I could be transferred (upon entering the fifth grade) to my neighborhood public school, I had vast experience with the minor deities and demons (white and black) who paced or prowled the aisles, who cajoled or counseled, who bullied or corralled us with total authority within their own well ordered realm, their own particular spheres of influence. The moments that resonate most are, of course, those connected to drama.

Jane Neil School

I am eight years old and every morning before dawn cracks, I ride the yellow pick-up bus to Jane L. Neil School. Jane Neil sits on 87th and Indiana, worlds away from Morgan Park, the secure middle class Negro community where I live. It is across several neighborhood zones, if not actual time zones. I am in the third grade. I am in my seat, a too large lift-top desk second row from the window, fifth seat back. I am one of four Negro children (we were Negroes then)—three quiet handicapped brown boys and me—a tiny brown girl in a room seemingly filled with twenty-one shining plump and placid white crippled children, their crutches stowed beneath their seats, their unreliable limbs braced, their polio unseen and the muscle twitches caused by cerebral palsy momentarily stilled while they sit. It is late Friday afternoon in Miss Vigor's class. In fact, it is nearly two o'clock, almost time for the bell to ring; almost time for Miss Vigor to dismiss the class so that we can all line up to move outside to the bus dock, where we will line up again to board the buses that will carry us home.

My capacity to slip away from any immediate confining space has allowed me to anticipate the bell and freedom. Though I have already gone outside and beyond closed the window, daydreaming, and thus have been absent for a few moments of precious class time, I do know the correct time for I have just glanced at the clock and attempted to force my will on the mechanical universe: "Ring bell, ring! I want to go home now!" I shout silently to the clock. Though I do not read words well, I have learned to read the clock and so I know when it is nearly time to go. The clock, however, moves like Mississippi following *Brown v. the Board of Education;*—with all deliberate speed.

While she does not actually hear the subversive silent wish, Miss Vigor evidently reads the errant thought on my face, catches a quick glimpse of it half-hidden beneath my eyes. She is a fortyish, graying, stocky woman who can move with the speed of a snake in high grass. Sensing sedition, she strikes. She stoops at my desk, her hard stubby white fingers grabbing at my chin. She pulls her puffy gray heavy-jowled face within inches of mine. I smell the garlic on her breath, see

37

her broad nostrils flare and her tiny gray eyes narrow more as she attacks, pinching my cheeks, twisting my face around to meet hers. "Why are you staring at that clock?" she demands. "You need every minute in this class to learn! Why, you still can't even read." And then she adds what was meant to be the devastating blow designed to crush me should I ever again think about rebellion. "You," she hisses venomously to me and the listening class, "are dumb and stupid. You will never amount to anything because *you cannot read.*" Certain of her victory, Miss Vigor then let my face go and slithered back to the front of the room.

Miss Vigor's accusation did cause me to doubt my ability to read at that point. Perhaps I simply chose not to read for her. Perhaps, because I truly did not like her, I unconsciously selected the role of the quintessential resisting reader. Or, perhaps because I was, as family oral history has repeatedly maintained, a maddeningly deliberate child—slow to move, slow to dress, slow to eat—I was also slow to read in so discomforting a setting. You need to understand: My vaunted temperate pace at home had attained the status of legend. Daddy, who needed to be at the CTA bus barn by 5:30 every morning, was assigned the job of waking me up, helping me to dress, and giving me breakfast before the school bus arrived every morning. One day, totally frustrated by my capacity to daydream while dressing, he shifted the task back to Mama, declaring with exasperation, "she could drive a crazy man crazy." It wasn't that I was a terribly willful child, rather it was more that I simply was not encumbered by the urgencies of the present moment; and so I had the capacity to drift into interior space while pulling on my socks. Other adults were equally perplexed by my pace. "My God," they marveled, "she's as slow as molasses in January." A phrase that lived with me like a ghost in the walls of a haunted house.

I may well have been exceedingly relaxed with respect to movement, eating and dressing at a snail's pace, but I was neither "dumb" nor "stupid." Had that been the case, why would my second grade teacher, the pretty, vivacious, Miss Johnson, select me as the chosen one, the trusted designated runner with permission to leave the class to deliver messages to the front office or to other teachers? (Now, it could also be that I was less encumbered than many of my peers, having neither wheelchair, crutches, nor leg-braces to impede my progress. All things being relative, I was, therefore, despite my much maligned lack of speed, much faster than anyone else there!) Did I merely deduce my destination by the number on an office or classroom door, or by the colorful placards and bulletin boards that lined the halls? How could I, in the second grade, determine where I was to go with my valuable messages *if I could not read*? I had certainly developed a system of successfully finding my way, but whole word recognition seemed to play only a muted part. Rather, I employed memory, intuition, basic instinct, or plain interrogation. "Where is Miss Dawkins room?" I might ask a hall monitor who saw me casually meandering down the wide spacious halls.

Christmas at Grandmothers

So yes. There may well have been some truth to the initial charge, "you cannot read." Or, careful attention to reading may well have been a convenience for me, a skill I either employed or ignored as circumstances warranted.

Take for instance, the strained Christmas that my mother, brother and I spent in Los Angeles, at my Grandmother's home, the year I turned seven. This particular Christmas, which ended in abject disaster for all of us, was spent away from my Daddy, our friends, and Chicago's Christmas Eve snow (how, my brother and I fretted, could Santa Claus land without snow?). Grandmother's magnificent Washington Square home, to us a huge mansion complete with servants quarters and four bathrooms! (if no actual servants) was the center, the hive of Christmas day activity for her extended family. Grandmother was the queen bee and all of her sons, with all of their children, would come for Christmas dinner and to celebrate the joy of the day that very afternoon. The day before, my mother, Grandmother's oldest child, had been shopping and baking and otherwise helping Grandmother and my Aunt Louvenia, my Mama's only sister, prepare for a family Christmas. My brother and I had been told to be good, to be on our "best behavior." We had been instructed to always say "Grandmother," and never to slip and say "Grandma" or "Granny" when our many cousins arrived. We were told not "to behave like barbarians" but as respectful guests in Grandmother's home. To ease our tremendous worry, it had also been explained that Santa would know where to find us and the mystery of how he could land had been cleared up. "See Sweetie," Mama told me, "he puts wheels on the sleigh to make visits in California." (I promptly communicated this vital information to my brother). On Christmas eve, we had been firmly told to go to bed and not to wake the whole house up when we rose on Christmas morning.

That fateful morning, at about 5:30, we arose and crept down the wide panelled staircase, silently as ordered. The towering white-flocked Christmas tree in Grandmother's huge sitting area/den, which had been empty the night before, was now positively overburdened with stacks and stacks of gaily wrapped presents in all kinds of vivid colors and tinseled foil ribbons with attached paper tags. Not at all like the modest assortment of basic red and green colored packages Santa left wrapped around our presents in Chicago. Tanny, my brother, had always gotten red packages while mine were always wrapped in green. But here in Los Angeles, at Grandmother's house, presents spilled from beneath that tree from all sides in tumultuous cascades of vivid color. We had never seen so much loot and it was all ours! We were the only kids in the house! Santa had really missed us in Chicago and was making up for it here!

It wasn't until I unwrapped the fourth doll that I began to sense that something was wrong. Santa had never before left me more than one doll at a time. And although I appreciated his new found generosity, I began to suspect that something wasn't quite right. Suppose Santa had made a mistake? My suspicions raised, I put the question aloud to my big brother. More cautious now, he too, began to slow the frantic, heroic effort to quietly, quickly but efficiently tear open every package beneath the beautiful tree.

When the adults in the house, my Grandmother, my stylish Hollywood Aunt, and my mother, finally came downstairs later that morning, they took in the collateral damage to the tree—white flocking scattered in clumps around the room, the ripped and torn wrapping paper in mounds, the multitude of opened presents strewn haphazardly about the room while others lay half-stripped under the denuded tree, very much resembling debris from a hurricane—and promptly flew into a fiercesome rage.

"How could you?!" my Aunt almost screamed.

"What made you two do such a thing?" Grandmother demanded sternly with both hands on her hips, her gray-brown eyes hardening.

"Why didn't you just look at the name tags and take only your gifts?" they all wanted to know.

"Some of these gifts are for your cousins; they're going to be so hurt," they then informed us. At the end of the first salvo they wearily declaimed in unison, "you've made a huge mess!" Then they continued to glare and berate us for an eternity while stooping to pick up tissue paper, wrapping paper, bedraggled bows and ribbons. In truth, my grandmother and Aunt were far more distraught than Mama. She just looked at the mess we'd made, her Chicago gangsters come to call, shook her head with that familiar look of disgusted resignation and murmured, "I told you, I told you." To whom her comment was directed was never quite clear.

Under fire from the stinging barrage of questions and accusations, I felt unfairly attacked; after all, wasn't I the one who had stopped the stripping frenzy, sensing Santa had made an error? After being verbally bombarded for what seemed like hours, and the constant picking at our souls with the charge, "if they hadn't been so selfish and just read the name tags," from the corner where I had retreated I finally raised a tear-streaked face and struggled to defend myself with all the defiance I could summon.

"I don't know why you all are picking on me," I declared. "You know I can't read!"

42

"*You* will never amount to anything because *you cannot read.*" Miss Vigor's vicious accusation truly made me mad. And mine was a hard held anger that as a child I could hold and stoke until, like an iron falling upon soft skin, it scorched. Miss Vigor, with her squat menacing storm-cloud demeanor had clearly crossed the line, belittling me in front of the entire class. And though she spat her insults through clenched teeth, I heard them clearly as did everyone else. Of course, I could read. This woman would have to be shown. I was my mother's daughter; my Daddy's baby; I had heard since I could hear Mama's abiding precept that you never let anybody walk on you; you always gave 'em, as Mama always gave her adversaries, "a piece of my mind."

But, I would have to "bide my time," as Mama also said, for I could not launch a frontal attack. My teacher had pronounced me dumb; had insisted that I could not read and therefore would remain dumb. She must have the lie thrown back in her face. The next week, we began yet another boring educational treatise—*Fun With Dick and Jane*—featuring Sister Sally, Spot the dog and Puff the cat as supporting cast. This time, however, when called upon to read aloud to the class, I invested the voices of those limited blond stick children with a resonance and vibrancy they never before had held. While other children still haltingly hunted and pecked, stumbling over each declarative simple sentence heavy on the action verbs of "see," "look," and "run" ("Sally said see-the-cookies. Cookies-for Puff and Spot"), I infused each line with voice, giving each individual character and paragraph a new, if histrionic, potential. Sometimes I even reversed word order or injected other lines, interpolating the "action" to add what warmth and color one could to a sorry ass Dick and Jane, those limited sagas of supposed white domestic bliss. Pouring honey into my voice I'd read: "Sally said, 'See the cookies, Puff. Cookies for Puff and Spot. Cookies for Baby Tim. The big cookie is for Sally. Look and see Sally's cookie. See Sally's big, big cookie.' It is so so good. [Then] Jane said, 'See the pets. See the pets come to the house. See Sally's family run."

When I completed my assigned reading that day, neither Miss Vigor, nor anyone else in my class, could challenge me, laugh at me, or pick at me again. And though I believe it pained her, Miss Vigor moved me from the "C" list to the "A" list in reading. She gave me a gold star to carry home to my Mama, and she had to put my name on the bulletin board ahead of everyone else's, for I had become the top class reader, the one called upon to demonstrate how it should be done when other adults came to visit.

Now on those occasions when I struggle to understand why the Credit Union and I never can agree on my bank balance; or when I am trapped in a mind-numbing "budget adjustment" meeting with four other women, knowing I have little to offer beyond the pained plea, "Can't you just tell me the bottom line? How much can I spend?" *Knowing* that there is no math marker on my DNA, I often think of Miss Vigor. In these rare moments of reflection, I catch myself wishing the woman had shaken me twice, reflecting that had she just attacked my total disregard for basic addition or those mysterious times tables once you got past the fives, perhaps I could have risen to the challenge presented by arithmetic. As it is, however, math remains my one true handicap.

Jamel Shabazz

In The Beginning There Was the Word
Patrice Gaines

I was seven years old when I learned that you could write something so powerful it could change a person's mind.

I was in second grade in Quantico, Virginia, and I still wet the bed at night. Most Saturdays my mother propped the mattress from my twin bed against the backyard fence where everyone—including the teenaged boy I had a crush on–could see it.

"We have to air out that thing so it won't stink in here," my mother said to my father and he dutifully dragged the black and white mattress outside.

Besides me and my parents, the only other person in the house was my two-year-old sister, so I assumed all my friends knew who was responsible for the yellow stain in the middle of the mattress. Surely, they knew a child as small as my sister did not make a yellow ring the circumference of an aluminum bucket. I was frozen with shame. I stayed inside as long as I could, quiet, out of eyesight of my mother.

But she always came to my room and found me.

"Get outside and play," she ordered.

"It's hot," I complained.

She insisted, "It's Saturday. I don't care how hot it is."

I went outside, but never to the backyard until my father carried the mattress back inside.

This was in the days when people thought children who wet the bed were just too lazy to get up and go to the bathroom. Today, doctors tell parents there is a reason some children sleep so deeply they are not awakened by the urge to pee. When I was a kid, you got a whipping for wetting the bed, and I got plenty of them.

At night I tried not to fall asleep, but I always failed. My parents took me to the doctor for all kinds of tests. They bought a contraption that had a rubber mat for me to sleep on, which was connected to a machine that beeped as soon as water hit the mattress. I peed the first night and the alarm blared, waking up everyone in the house—except me. My baby sister was in my mother's arms crying, and my mother and father were leaning over me when I woke up.

"Pat, Pat, wake up," I heard my mother and father say in unison. I woke, startled, thinking I was dreaming. My parents discarded the machine and mat and we all waited on the next new treatment to appear. Then one night I got the idea to write a letter to God. I knew that my mother, a prayerful woman, paid attention to God. I knew my letter would get her attention:

> DEAR GOD,
>   PLEASE HELP ME. I DON'T WANT TO WET THE
> BED AND MAKE MY MOMMY BEAT ME.
>   LOVE, PAT

I placed the letter prominently on my dresser, where God and my mother could see it. Momma read it that night when she tucked me into bed. She turned to look at me, and I saw the sad look in her eyes. She never said anything about the letter—and she never beat me again either.

I knew when I wrote the letter that I could make her feel bad, but I never dreamed that a note on some lined notebook paper could make her stop beating me. After that incident I thought of words as magic. If they could make my mother stop beating me, what else could words do? I knew that I wanted to learn how to use them well enough to get whatever I wanted and needed.

Turn The Page and You Don't Stop!

Many years later, when I was a troubled teenager and believed I couldn't talk to anyone, I started secretly writing. I wrote long poems, stories, prose, letters to myself or letters I would never mail to boyfriends who hurt me. I didn't have to send the letters to reap the healing benefits of writing them. Every single word was carefully chosen to make a point and each one was like drops of blood from a wound that needed to bleed in order to heal.

I tucked the letters, and poems, and pages and pages of words away inside a drawer under my underwear, where no one would ever find them. I thought people would laugh at my words or think I was crazy.

When I was 23 years old I got a job as a secretary at a newspaper and made friends with another woman my age, Cynthia. We shared peanut butter and jelly sandwiches at lunchtime and we told each other our secrets.

"I want to become a marine biologist one day," Cynthia whispered to me one day.

"I want to be a writer," I said.

"I need to go back to school," she said.

"I need to keep writing," I said.

"You write?"

I let her question hang as I went over in my head what I had just said. I couldn't believe I had told her about my dream of becoming a writer. After that Cynthia asked me every day for two weeks to bring some of my poems so she could read them. I wouldn't even consider showing them to anyone else, but finally one day I brought in my book of poems to show her.

She read them slowly and carefully at lunch. "I love them," she said.

"You do?" I was astounded.

As far as I was concerned she was looking at me naked. She saw my birth mark and scars, my varicose veins and stretch marks.

"They make me think about my own life," she said.

"They do?"

Cynthia was white; I was black. She was married; I was single. She didn't have any children; I had a daughter. I wrote about being loved and left. I wrote about being a mother who was afraid she didn't know how to raise a child. I wrote about wanting to be more than I was.

"We're so much alike," she said.

I was astounded again. As I fell asleep that night, I thought about what she had said, until just as I was about to doze off I got it. Words are like musical notes. The power is in how you arrange them. You can write them down in a way that shows people the answers they need for their own lives. The melody is familiar to them. It reminds them of something, though they may not even know what it is.

I knew then that I could offer someone an escape with my words. I could tickle them along the way and make the journey more pleasant. If I put the words in the right order I could make the differences between people disappear.

After my mother stopped beating me for wetting the bed, I started reading a lot. I read fairy tales and stories: *Tom Sawyer, King Arthur, Rebecca of Sunnybrook Farm.* I read for pure fun. Reading was like a meditation for me, though I didn't know it at the time. I *saw* Tom Sawyer. I *heard* King Arthur. I *was* with Rebecca. Even today, when I read, the world disappears and I step inside the book.

Turn The Page and You Don't Stop!

I will never forget a woman who attended English and math classes with me at a community college. She had a terrible habit of cursing, especially if she got excited or upset. This habit made some people avoid her because they had seen her snap over what seemed like nothing in the middle of class and spit out a string of curse words that made even the street smart wince. I ignored her too, but mostly because I was busy trying to keep up in math, where she excelled.

"Can I talk to you?" she asked one day.

I paused.

She kept talking. "I was wondering if I could make a deal with you. I could tutor you in math if you would help me in reading and English."

I admit I was surprised. I didn't think she cared about English or school.

"I have a bad habit of cursing," she said.

I held in my laughter.

"I curse because I get frustrated because I don't know some of the words in the reading. And then when I want to explain, I end up cursing because I can't think of right word to express my feelings. I need to increase my vocabulary. I think if I knew more words, I would use them."

"I never thought of that," I said, thinking out loud about how it made sense that if you read more you learned more words. Then, when you needed those words, you could reach for them.

Of course, I agreed to tutor her. We helped each other for two years. She tutored me in math, thank goodness. I passed math and she learned to read better, enough to enjoy books. She passed English—and eventually, stopped cursing so much. People stopped avoiding her and realized she was a smart and funny woman.

I think of her sometimes when I look at the black and white photo I have in my office entitled "Reading" and described as "Former slave learning to read." It is the photo of one black woman sitting in a chair with an open book in her lap while another black woman stands by her, one arm across her shoulder, pointing with her other hand to something in the book. They are poor and in tattered, dirty clothes, sitting outside on a porch. I imagine after hours of working they steal time to read.

I don't allow myself to forget that slaves were not allowed to learn to read, or that some people risked their lives to try. Or that the women in my photo took seriously the freedom to read; that they understood that people who can read will not be slaves.

WHY CAN'T DANTE READ?
AN APPEAL TO BLACK PARENTS
David Miller

Year after year we are bombarded with reports and media portrayals of the growing achievement gap between Black and White students. Much discussion and debate over the causes have yielded few solutions.

While Asian students continue to excell academically and outpace other groups in graduate school admissions at many of the finer universities throughout the nation, · the question in the Black community remains: Why can't Dante read? Many would cite poor and failing schools and uncertified teachers to explain the phenomenon. Others cite lack of parental involvement in making sure that Black children come to school ready to learn. Whatever the case, Black students continue to lag far behind expectations when it comes to academic pursuits.

Within Black communities, dropout rates are increasing; poor reading skills and unsatisfactory scores on standardized test have prompted Black parents across the country to seek strategies to improve academic outcomes for children and youth. More and more Black families are realizing that they have the power to close the achievement gap.

In today's society Black families have greater access to educational technology, quality after school experiences and culturally relevant books and other materials. *Amazing Grace, Justin and the Best Biscuits in the World, Mufaro's Beautiful Daughters, Charlie Pippin, Aunt Harriet's Underground Railroad in the Sky* and *Her Stories:*

African American Folktales, Fairytales, and True Tales are among the plethora of book titles available for beginning readers which feature empowering images of Black children. The emergence of Black books for children and teenagers underscores the need for Black parents to recognize literacy as a key to success.

Unfortunately, reading and academic excellence no longer seem to be a priority in many homes within the Black community. It's troubling to admit that too many Black parents are allowing Dante's intellectual potential to atrophy as he spends hours manipulating a "joy stick" playing "Grand Theft Auto", "John Madden NFL Football" or any of the other latest handheld video games to reach the store shelves. If Dante has no books in his room but has a television, access to all of the latest video games ("Play Station", "X Box", etc), and a cell phone, it is no wonder that he is preoccupied with things he believes to be more interesting than reading.

The charge for Black parents must be to introduce reading to children early and often. According to *America's Children: Key National Indicators of Well Being,* 2002, reading aloud to children helps them develop the prerequisite skills they will need to learn in school. Being read to has been identified as a source of a child's early literacy development, including knowledge about the alphabet, print and characteristics of written language." Introducing nursery rhymes and rhyming games to toddlers and young children exposes them early to the joys of reading. Through the use of the internet and trips to your local library parents can locate books for older readers. Finding materials that are developmental appropriate, culturally relevant as well as books that spark interest and curiosity in youth are critical to provide children with meaningful reading experiences that are fun and educational.

One example of finding books written by Black authors that might interest older readers is *Monster*, written by the celebrated Black author Walter Dean Myers. The book is an exciting memoir about the life of a 16 year old boy on trial for murder. The story dramatizes the moral dilemmas and difficult decisions faced by adolescent males.

How can we expect Dante to excel if he continues spending more hours playing video games and watching Rap City verses exploring the joys of learning through reading?

When we examine the current plight of Black children and youth in schools throughout this nation, it is clear that we have taken our "eyes off the prize." According to the National Black Child Development Institute, a non-profit advocacy group based in Washington, D.C., an alarming 60 % of African American 4th graders cannot read at grade level. These startling statistics illuminate the growing need for Black parents to play a more active role in developing a generation of Black children and youth who have a thirst for reading and academic excellence.

With a rich history of academic and literacy contributions that can be traced over 10,000 years from the Meter Du Neter (Hieroglyphics) in the tombs of Luxor in ancient Kemit (Egypt) to the early literary contributions of David Walker's *Appeal to The Colored Citizens of the United States* in 1829, Black people have always placed a great deal of emphasis on education as a tool for social, spiritual and political advancement. This can be evidenced by major literary movements like the Harlem Renaissance and the Black Arts Movements of the 1920s and 1960s respectively. The Harlem Renaissance produced giants like W.E.B. DuBois, Langston Hughes, Claude McKay and Zora Neal Hurston; while the Black Arts movement produced playwrights, poets and intellectual critics like Leroy Jones (Amiri Baraka), Don L.Lee (Haki R. Madhubuti), Sonia Sanchez, and Harold Cruse.

This history is exemplified in the lives of so many Blacks who struggled during slavery, reconstruction, segregation and Jim Crow to achieve educational excellence despite the social as well legal structures that denied them equity. Perhaps one of the best examples is John Johnson, the founder and publisher of *Ebony Magazine*. *Ebony Magazine* provided "Black Folks" with something to read as well as a blue print for Black self help. With a circulation of over 2.7 million readers world wide, *Ebony* educated a generation of people through literacy as a tool for advancement. *Ebony's* insightful articles over the years educated generations of Black folks. It provided a written legacy which covered everything from the 1954 landmark *Brown v. Board of Education* Decision to the historic Million Man March of 1995. *Ebony* increased our collective awareness of the power of reading and documenting our story for the world. "The reason I succeeded was that I didn't know that it was impossible to succeed" are the immortal words of John Johnson. His legacy provides the Black community with a foundation for understanding the importance of reading as a key to self-empowerment.

Although the task may seem daunting, millions of Black parents are successfully raising healthy, productive and literate children in some of the most horrific social conditions in the U.S. and abroad. Black parents are the backbone of the community, thus as we begin to find "new" ways to educate, train and empower our children through a renewed sense of academic excellence and vision creation, we can improve the vitality of the Black community.

TURN THE PAGE AND YOU DON'T STOP!

Whether your child attends a public school, private school, charter school or home school, promoting reading in your home is essential. Most would agree that homes which promote literacy and high academic standards are more likely to create children and youth who have a greater sense of their self worth and are able to conceptualize a vision for the future. Often this vision includes college and business ownership.

If we are serious about making sure "Dante can read," we must begin to promote a value system in the home that encourages high academic standards and expectations for excellence. Within the Black community mediocrity can no longer be the norm!

Finally, the following are five things that Black parents can do to increase interest in reading and academic potential:

I. Understand that your home is your child's first classroom. Thus, as a parent, your role is to make sure you monitor the information that your children receive.

2. Turn the television OFF! Create fun yet educational relevant assignments for your children. During the school year reduce the amount of television your children watch daily. BET and MTV can no longer be used as devices to baby sit children and youth.

3. Encourage your child to read more at home. Make reading part of your leisure activities. If you want your child to get excited about reading, make sure you read! Make time to read with your child. You cannot be too busy or too tired for this important part of parenting.

4. Check your child's homework. Create a schedule for homework. Agree on a time and space in your home to get the homework completed and reviewed. When your child comes home without homework encourage him or her to read interesting articles in books and magazines. Ask questions, engage them in conversations. This interested inter-action will help them to improve reading and com-prehension skills.

5. Talk to your children about their school day. Dinner time is a great time for sharing. It is also important to listen to your child without judging.

NERD BY NATURE: PROUD BY CHOICE
Cory Anderson

When I was a kid, I hated being called a "nerd," but I clearly fit the "80s" definition. I wore glasses that seemed to be perpetually broken in one way or another. I was "smart" in all the traditional ways. And I read everything I could get my hands on. Nerdiness was my calling card. Nerdiness was seemingly my lot in life. And yet, that nerdiness paid off in ways that I could have never expected as a 12 year old trying to figure out a smooth comeback when my cousins made fun of my "coke bottle" glasses.

Intellectualism in Black youth is even today sometimes met with various forms of derision. Growing up in the 1970s and early 1980s, I learned first hand the dangers of being perceived as "too smart" by your peer group. My father was in the military and only by chance, I spent my pre-school years in Germany. At that time, my father was a low ranking, non-commissioned officer so there was nothing special about our time there. We didn't really "experience" Europe as you might imagine, we simply lived there while he was stationed there. I actually started school in Germany, attending kindergarten with other military kids and our German counterparts who were learning English as a second language.

After that time in Europe, my family spent several years in Denver before my parents' divorce landed me in the original chocolate city, Gary, Indiana. In the midst of all that moving, I turned out to be a pretty smart kid with a natural attraction to the written word. So, at 12, I was too smart and I wore thick glasses. I was a nerd in the city, and an easy target for peers who didn't understand, who didn't see the value and who, understandably, were put off by what seemed to them to be an air of superiority.

Early in my teen years, Richard Wright, James Baldwin and Ralph Ellison provided a clearer context for the society into which we all had been born. All three of these writers told stories that explained in clear terms the connection between how Black men were treated in society and how Black men many times responded to that treatment. As a young person, that knowledge was mentally liberating. All three of them demonstrated both in their writing and in their own lives that Black men could not be defined nor limited by stereotypes or societal expectations. For me, that was an important realization.

On the other side of the spectrum, J.R.R. Tolkien helped me to transcend my surroundings and explore worlds beyond my limited surroundings. I had read and re-read Tolkien's *Lord of the Rings* Trilogy long before the movie. Having read them made the experience of sharing the movie with my own family that much more rewarding. Tolkien helped me to better appreciate the constant struggle between good and evil and how even fantasy literature can have real world applications. In that same way, Stephen King, master of literary horror, helped to illuminate for me the power of storytelling. The idea that words could evoke such powerful and real emotions, fear in King's case, was another factor that encouraged my love of the written word.

Eventually, the nerdiness wore off. By the time I made it to high school, young people had begun to actually appreciate the value of a certain level of intellectualism, at least as far as it made high school work easier. And by college, smart was in. Smart was suddenly sexy, being well read made you attractive. Nerdiness suddenly paid good dividends.

Turn The Page And You Don't Stop!

It was at some point during that time that I connected my years of reading with the ability to actually write. It makes perfect sense now. I had read millions of words in thousands of possible configurations, words that were intended to excite, sadden, titillate, inform, educate and evoke hundreds of other different responses. It follows that after reading all of those words that I should have been able to write in a similar way. Granted, Ellison I was not, but I could be Ellison—like when I tried. I couldn't tell stories like Stephen King but I had an appreciation for the power of first person narrative that infused what I wrote. Reading and writing were naturally connected and the more I wrote, the more I wanted to read.

In college, the path of least resistance for me was Journalism. I studied, and learned the craft of writing to inform and persuade. Probably the most important thing that I learned was that the best journalists, the most prolific and compelling writers, were also ferocious readers. And while my ferocity did not necessarily guarantee my success as a writer, it did give me a measure of confidence. If I did nothing more than try to emulate the best of what I had read, I would at least become a competent writer.

I hope that I've become more than just competent. Writing (and reading) have become for me the basis a fulfilling career working to bring a measure of justice to under-served families in this world. I worked for a year as a professional journalist exploring the inter-section between education, opportunity and youth violence in our communities. That year of journalism has turned into over a decade of work in this area. The first half of that decade involved writing about, mentoring and developing programs for kids for whom the street gang served as family. In recent years I have used my skills to help support community based programs; I have also worked in philanthropy to direct resources toward the critical needs of struggling kids and families. How have I done these things? First, I read to learn; second, I interact and act; third, I write to inform and compel others to action.

Jamel Shabazz

Free Public Libraries:
Democracy's Real Test
Haki R. Madhubuti

My voracious reading habit and the lack of friends as a child accompanied me into adulthood. Coming up, I was always a stranger in my own home. I developed quite early the practice of reading any and everything in a cultural environment where reading was not encouraged or rewarded by family, friend, or teachers. I read newspapers, dream books, racing forms, magazines, the Bible, books forced on us in elementary school, and those books denied me by adults because of my age. When I discovered the Detroit Children's Library and Detroit's Main Public Library at the age twelve, it was like hitting the numbers (today's lottery). There, I was the perpetual winner.

Unlike most of the young white students that visited the Detroit Public Library in the 1950s I was not able to attach myself to a librarian who would help guide my reading. There were not any Black librarians on or near the main desk with whom I could connect. Often, the white librarians, mostly women- viewed my constant visits as a dilemma. This was during the time of America's Apartheid. My presence was barely tolerated and generally ignored.

My mother was very much dysfunctional at this time. Her drinking and drug-addiction had taken over her life. Most of her days and nights were devoted to looking for the next high. My father was an absent entity who surfaced in extreme emergencies—and then just to drop a few coins peppered with lots of criticism. The Detroit Public Library became a home away from home, a place where I could briefly leave the harsh realities of my days and nights.

Turn The Page and You Don't Stop!

Like most poor people we moved almost yearly, relocating in the same general area because of the restricted living spaces for Black folks. As a young boy, I viewed this as luck. It kept me in the same schools and I stayed in walking distance of the main library. The library became my intellectual refuge and a point of cultural departure and stability in my young life.

I outgrew the children's library rather quickly and began frequenting the adult library while in elementary school. Before I started Junior High, I knew the ins and outs of the main library like the back streets of Detroit I maneuvered to get there. A young boy without street attachment (gangs or youth groups) meant that I had to be very careful about where I walked. I learned quickly. My routes became second nature. Almost intuitively, I knew the best time of day it was safe to walk in certain areas. I developed all kinds of shortcuts and detours that allowed me to be as anonymous as possible. A young boy with an arm full of books was always ripe for ridicule, attack or recruitment by local gangs.

I was somewhat known in the area because my mother was a popular barmaid at one of the notorious nightspots. I was my mother who encouraged me to read. Even in the deepest part of her sickness she understood that I needed much more than the public schools could provide. Also, my sister, a year and a half younger than I, was one of the "finest" girls in the city. Because of her I experienced a rather dubious distinction. First, most of the older boys wanted to meet her and would approach me for an introduction. Second, when she didn't want to be bothered, she would use me to threaten them. "If you don't leave me alone, I'll tell my brother," she'd say.

Often I had to fight and run my way to and from school. This forced me to carry all kinds of weapons: kitchen knives and broken door locks that I would use like brass knuckles. I was attacked often. At six-feet one-inch and weighing one hundred and forty pounds, I, a light-skinned "Negro," did not strike fear into the hearts of my peers. I was forced to learn rather quickly how to talk or "signify" my way out of most street situations. This use of language as a means of protection started early in my life, and my familiarity with language and literature, specifically Black literature, helped tremendously.

A good many of the local gang members were poor students and required help with exams and papers, and I would either sell my services or offer them free, depending on the circumstances. This helped me only among the "brothers" who were still in school. By the time they reached high-school age, most of the gang members had decided that street employment was more lucrative in the short run than sitting in dull classrooms six hours a day listening to teachers who felt imprisoned themselves. The Detroit (and later Chicago) Public Library aided me to no end in supplementing my education. The card catalog was my early world wide web. I had at my finger tips the key to where all the books were.

Most of my homework was completed in the public library. Acquiring an "A" average in junior high was not difficult in this environment. It was also rather deceptive in measuring my own intelligence because the I.Q. bar had been lowered far below the best schools in the system. Obviously, I was not aware of this at the time and only began to understand my un-preparedness when I was admitted to one of the best high schools in the state of Michigan, Cass Tech.

TURN THE PAGE AND YOU DON'T STOP!

Cass Tech in the late 1950s was a magnet school that attracted the best students from the neighborhood schools. Students had to have a minimum of a "B" average to take the admissions exam. Cass was unusual in that it was both a technical school and primarily a college prep institution. Each student majored in a particular field. Since I was a half-way decent trumpet player in junior high (and since I was without any counseling) I chose music as my major.

My frequent visits to the Detroit Public Library helped me to endure my year at Cass Tech, a highly racist school that taught me that I was not wanted and that I needed to understand this system in order to be competitive. I lived in an environment where I made all the important decisions about my life. No one else in my family was in a position to advise me. I left Cass Tech after my freshman year for a neighborhood high school because I didn't have a support system and my situation at home had gotten considerably worse. My mother's drug habit had completely taken over her life. My sister, now fourteen, was pregnant by one of the major gang leaders in Detroit. This was a catastrophe. During those days, it was considered taboo for girls to have children outside of traditional marriage.

As the "man" of the house, I went looking for the father to uphold the "honor" of our home. I found him and confronted him with her pregnancy, which he didn't deny. I commenced to try and break his jaw, a move not in my best interest, but consistent with the code of the streets. Even if I was not physically equipped to enforce it, I had to do what was expected of the "men" at that time. I endured one of the worse beatings a boy of sixteen could tolerate from a twenty-year-old man. Upon returning home and explaining my bruised and disfigured face to my slightly inebriated mother, I received another whipping for getting whipped.

I left home that Saturday afternoon and went to the only place in my young life that I knew would not be critical of me or my actions, the Detroit Public Library. I remember locating Mark Twain's *The Adventures of Huckleberry Finn* on the shelves and finding a quiet place to read. I lost myself in the fiction of a white progressive writer who tried to paint some Black and whites as victims of a culture and nation that they had no control over. After three hours of reading with a few naps in between, I left the library feeling that my life had changed considerably. In the fast-changing world, I had a few more choices to control my destiny than "Nigger Jim"; literature had taught me that, and the two whippings I experienced that day confirmed in my young mind the realities of my life.

The year was 1958 and I had accepted, even within the critical climate of racism, that free public libraries would be in my life forever. As I walked home that Saturday evening with two books under my arms, it hit me that all I needed to acquire vast quantities of knowledge about the world was a library card—which was free. On that day, even the white librarians had softened their responses to me. As I checked out the books, quiet and unassuming but clearly wounded physically and psychologically, their smiles denoted for the first time in four years, welcome.

During the walk home, my short life passed in front of me. I now accepted the hard fact that I was on my own and the only thing that would protect me was my superior knowledge base. This knowledge would allow me personal and professional options other than the streets. For a poor Black boy, the free public library was my equalizer and the best example of real democracy at work for poor people who lacked the resources to buy all the books they needed or desired.

Turn The Page And You Don't Stop!

During these early years, I started collecting books. Most of the clothes I wore were bought at second hand Salvation Army stores. At all of the Salvation Army stores, there were book sections where hundreds of books and magazines were available at a fraction of the list price. I remember finding first editions of work by Frank Yerby, Richard Wright, and W.E.B. DuBois and others for fifteen to twenty-five cents each. For ten cents, I acquired a used copy of *Rising Above Color* edited by Phillip Henry Lotz; the importance of this collection was that the editor had essays by George Washington Carver, Marian Anderson, W.E.B. DuBois, Samuel Coleridge-Taylor, Richard Allen, Fredrick Douglass, Paul Laurence Dunbar, James Weldon Johnson and others. This was an early introduction to the original thinking and to the complexity of some of our most talented people. Before the 1950s ended, I had quite a collection numbering about one hundred and ten books. To this day, second-hand book stores remain one of my favorite places to visit and collect my thoughts as well as good books.

In 1959 my mother was dead, my sister's son was close to a year old, and her son's father had abandoned his responsibility to pursue other women and the street life of Detroit, Michigan. I left Detroit via the Greyhound bus for Chicago (where my father lived) to begin a new life. I quickly found the Hall Branch Library at 48th and Michigan Avenue which had one of the most comprehensive collections of Black Literature, history and culture. I was in my last year of high school and finished a two-year program at Chicago's Dunbar Vocational High School in one year and a summer partially because of my intellectual center, acquired by outside reading. The Hall Branch Library had two Black librarians who helped me. Vivian Harsh, the head librarian, was receptive and helpful. However, it was Charlemae H. Rollins who helped to guide my reading and encouraged me to write my little poems. I had grown into an assiduous reader. "Never leave home without a book" was my mantra. A habit that has served me well. Today, reading is just as important as eating and sleeping.

The free library system of America, along with public schools remain the cornerstones and hope for poor and middle-class people, newly arrived immigrants and all citizens who value freedom. In the final countdown, the availability of life-giving, life-saving, and life-affirming knowledge levels the playing field for millions of folks systematically locked out of this system. For me, libraries—and the information they contain and freely share—represent the real liberated zones of this nation. When public education is compromised, and the budget and staff hours of public libraries are severely reduced, we are, indeed, in trouble.

Bond with your children by visiting public libraries regularly. Proudly, with them, use your library cards and with them especially with the very young, do the one thing that guarantees to elevate and free their minds: read, read and read. Whatever your next move is, your local library may help you on the journey.

FULL CIRCLE
Melrita Bonner

As a young girl, one of the things I looked forward to most was spending Saturdays with my mother. Most Saturdays, we'd drop my father off at work, then go to Community Bakery to buy an assortment of goodies including rye bread (to be eaten later with chili), doughnuts, chocolate cake and pocket book rolls. Next, we'd do the grocery shopping at Safeway. Then, we'd go home to eat and afterwards, we'd head out to the Ivey Branch Library.

The Ivey Branch Library was the "colored library," an oversized room where discarded/withdrawn items were routinely sent from the big public library downtown. Many of these books were clearly stamped or marked and those of us who checked out books usually knew that we were getting the stuff that "they" no longer wanted. The condition of the books was not good enough for "them" but we should just be glad to get them, I suppose, was the general idea. I developed a love of reading at an early age and was also taught at an early age that education/literacy would serve as the vehicle which would enable me to realize my goals and fulfill my responsibilities to society.

So, long story short, I read those books and I read those books and I read those books some more. One time, I got on a streak of reading books written by Grace Livingston Hill. There seemed to be tons of them and I read them and re-read them. Nice, clean grownup books with innocuous little stories that any mother would love for her young daughter to read. Never mind that none of the characters ever looked, acted, or lived like me or my family or friends. I kept reading and getting better at it and I kept learning about different stuff and people and places. I felt as though the world was my oyster.

Well, I grew up, went away to college, married, moved to another state, taught school, then moved back to my hometown. So, twenty-five years later, I was back home enjoying my family and friends and I decided that rather than teach, I wanted to make use of the Library Science degree I'd earned. I wanted to be a librarian and felt that being one would be the job for me. I applied for a job at the Little Rock Public Library. I got the job and made great strides as I relished the obvious perks of learning new things and being around books so much of the time.

Imagine my surprise—and delight—when, after a period of time I discovered a curious fact. I became aware that a good number of readers, (mostly female), constantly checked out the nice, clean type of books written in the style of Grace Livingston Hill. Although there are several authors who write books like Hill's, by far, those by Hill were the most popular. I noticed that some of those books were stamped "Ivey Branch Library." They had been circulating from the bookmobile and were now in high demand and heavily circulating at the main library. So, imagine, if you will, the dance I danced, the laugh I laughed, the high five I high fived and the thoughts I thought as I remembered checking out these very same books from the "colored library" all those years ago.

Now, all these years later, I thought about how reading those books played a significant part in giving me a firm grip on future goals and, simultaneously, making me aware that I had a duty to put forth the best effort in any task put before me. Reading those books helped me learn to work in order to excel. Setting that pattern rewarded me accordingly. Those old books had come full circle from being dis-

71

cards/withdrawns to being highly circulated to becoming discards (due to wear and tear) again and I was soaring in a job and living a lifestyle that I very much enjoyed. The old leftover books that had been sent to what was fondly referred to as the "Ivey Branch" had, one could say, served a purpose.

IF YOU WANT TO LEARN THE SECRETS OF THE WORLD, READ A BOOK!
Andrew P. Jackson (Sekou Molefi Baako)

Reading and the written word have been critical priorities for Black people throughout our time in this country. Our ancestors braved cruel and inhuman punishment and even death for learning to read or being caught with a book during enslavement. With the end of America's slavery in 1864, education and reading were one of our most cherished forms of freedom, especially for those living in southern states. In addition to public schools, many prestigious black colleges and universities were established during that period. During Reconstruction, (1865-1868), schools and teachers were respected for the roles both played in instilling skills that provided African Americans an opportunity to compete and succeed in society. Throughout the civil rights years, education was the prize and books were always the key.

Twenty-five years ago, I accepted a position at the first public institution named for Langston Hughes upon his death in 1967, the Langston Hughes Community Library and Cultural Center of the Queens Public Library, in New York City. This position would begin my true life's journey in librarianship. Prominent among my early memories is a statement by one of my colleagues during my orientation on service to our community. *"If you want to keep a secret from black people, put it in a book,"* he said. I questioned this statement because it was contrary to how I had been raised in a household that promoted reading and instilled an enjoyment of both books and education. However, over the years, through observation, study and public interaction, I've reluctantly accepted this to be truer than I would ever have expected.

Our mother was an elementary school music teacher and father was a statistician with the U.S. Army Corps of Engineers. He transferred to New York City around 1942 from Vicksburg, Mississippi, to make a better life for his family. Although Mom received her college degree from Tougaloo College, it was still illegal for her to use the local public library. My older brother and sister were born in Vicksburg, but attended local public schools in the Bedford-Stuyvesant section of Brooklyn. I'm the oldest of the Jackson triplets, (two boys and a girl), born during the "blizzard of 47," to the surprise of everyone. Everyone knew a baby was coming, but certainly not triplets. (This was long before modern medical technology.) We lived in a brownstone on Bainbridge Street off Ralph Avenue, until houses on our side of the street were demolished, in the early 1950s, to make room for a housing development. We moved to Curtis Street and 29th Avenue in East Elmhurst, Queens, and lived there until all of us were grown and on our own.

Mom enrolled us in to the Book-of-the-Month Club to ensure books were available for us to read as children. My favorites were *Robin Hood* (I still have that copy), *The Count of Monte Cristo* and *The Man in the Iron Mask.* It was not until I was grown that I learned the author, Alexandre Dumas, was a Black man. During the summers, we read several hours each day before we could go out to play, and shared what we read to our parents over dinner. On our thirteenth birthday, my older brother gave me a copy of Langston Hughes' *Simple Stakes a Claim.* Inside the cover, Walter wrote, "I hope you learn who Langston Hughes is." Ironically, twenty years later, I began my tenure as director of our local library. Since then, I have learned who he is, studied his life and works, and written about and lectured on his literary accomplishments. I now believe *The Creator's* master plan was for this particular library to be at the core of my transition.

Although I enjoyed reading, I was not a good student through high school. Immediately after graduating from high school, I served four years in the U.S. Air Force. From that experience, I learned discipline and was conditioned to challenge things I was told I could not accomplish. This was key, as I was constantly told by counselors that I was "not college material" throughout my school years. The new challenge was to prove them all wrong. After my discharge in 1968, I worked for the City of New York and attended CUNY's Baruch College in the evening. There, I received my first "A" grade ever, and knew if I earned one, I could repeat it. By 1980, I had completed 60 credits of my baccalaureate business program.

Once settled in my position at the Langston Hughes Library, I was asked to complete my studies towards my degree. The first course at York College (CUNY) was an African American Studies class that also introduced me to the extensive black heritage collection at the Langston Hughes Library. Since completing my undergraduate degree, I still read to feed my passion for Africana studies. This began a never-ending thirst for knowledge that still exists today. Reading altered my understanding and consciousness, and gave me a respect for my people and our contributions to world civilization.

Today, I find it hard to understand when a young person tells me he or she doesn't like to read or finds it unnecessary. Across the country, too many students read far below grade level. Through observation, I find they read for necessity rather than for recreation or for the sheer pleasure of reading. Years ago, when I regularly presented black history lectures on Rikers Island Correctional Facility, I learned that most teen inmates read on a fourth grade reading level and nationally on a sixth grade level. Teens come to our public libraries today primarily for e-mail and Internet chat groups rather than to read or circulate a book. How limiting. As a result, across this country, public library branches in minority communities suffer from low circulation and this translates into insufficient budgets and even closure of community libraries.

There is, however, a bright light in this abyss, in a nation that professes to value education, but shows few visible signs for us to believe it. We should be encouraged because young people have developed a real interest with the spoken word. The hip hop generation has benefited from Russell Simmons' Def Poetry Jam, open mic nights and spoken word slams, as they also serve to spark new interest in language, reading and writing by many youth. When I've discussed my essay about "culture messengers" from Langston Hughes to Tupac Shakur, connecting our literary past to their hip hop present, the response has been very positive. After each class students gather to look at copies of Shakur's *The Rose that grew From Concrete, The Moments, the Minutes, the Hours: The Poetry of Jill Scott* by Jill Scott, *Tears for Water Songbook of Poems & Lyrics* by Alicia Keyes and *Inside A Thug's Heart* by Angela Ardis.

For the past fifteen years, I've promoted reading, use of libraries and offered black history lectures to students from elementary grades to college level. These informational lectures fill the void in teacher lesson plans and offer alternatives for learning that teachers find difficult to include in a limited curriculum. As schools offer limited exposure to black writers and poets, students don't learn about the Harlem Renaissance of the 1920s or the Black Arts Movement of the 1960s. Thus, today's Spoken Word movement stands on the shoulders of earlier generations. It's our responsibility to educate some, remind others and encourage a new generation of Langston's and Nikki's, Baldwin's and Morrison's of their past.

In late June, I attended the annual conference of the American Library Association in Chicago. I had the opportunity to hear two excellent keynote speeches by Senator Barack Obama and best selling author Michael Eric Dyson. Both spoke of the impact books and libraries had on their lives, how they were exposed to a world outside of their immediate and limited environments of Hawaii and Detroit. This was not unlike the new world that opened to an illiterate Malcolm Little, who read and copied the dictionary and read every book in the prison library in order to properly express himself to the Honorable Elijah Muhammad. Each of these men learned the power of the written word and how critical reading and books are in the transformation of one's life.

For me, books transformed me into a student of Africana history for life. Although I am a professional librarian, lecturer, adjunct and writer, there are so many more books to read; there is so much more to learn.

Our ancestors suffered too much for the blessings and opportunities we have today. How can our youth not take advantage of them? When all else in our personal worlds appears to be closing in on us, a library card away is a book that will expand our universe and remind us of the wonders we have yet to behold.

"As I read, my ears are opened to the magic of the spoken word."

—Richard Wright

WRITING AND RESPONSIBILITY: A PERSONAL VIEW
D. H. Melhem Ph.D.

Amiri Baraka once noted that all writing is political—even writing that avoids it, like poems created as random words designed on a page. The avoidance itself is political, says Baraka. He's probably right. Of course, not all writers can shape words into acts of conscience. Rather than deliberate choices, the reasons may be those of temperament and capability. Still, convictions and opinions differ. And since writing itself is a gesture of free speech, we can expect a variety of responses to the same issues. Beyond expecting all citizens in a democracy to exercise their right to vote, we should make demands only on ourselves. Telling poets that they ought to be writing about political matters is like prescribing bad medicine. Hasty polemics make bad poetry that serves no cause well. And the results persist forever in print, often to the author's perpetual embarrassment.

I feel fortunate, however, in my own natural tendency to view life in its larger political and philosophical contexts. I have always wanted my writing to make a difference, to speak to its time. My own experience argues for a sensibility open to the human family, the global (and metaglobal) family to which we belong, and from which we draw our creative sustenance.

Years ago I noted that some of the best writers I knew, Black writers, were largely either unappreciated or misunderstood by the dominant culture. This realization helped me to focus my critical energies (and some of my poetry, too). As an only child reared in a large, multicultural family, I had learned early that a literature of beauty and nobility could be depreciated because it differed from the majority culture. I saw that in the United States, differences were often translated into deficiencies. I considered it a privilege to study the work of Gwendolyn Brooks, Dudley Randall, Sonia Sanchez, Haki R. Madhubuti, Jayne Cortez, and Amiri Baraka, a privilege to interview them, know them, and interpret the heroic qualities of their lives and works.

When no publisher welcomed my studies, each rejection became a challenge. Shaping my doctoral dissertation on Gwendolyn Brooks (1976, City University of New York) into a publishable manuscript and finding a publisher took over ten years, including many rejections. *Gwendolyn Brooks: Poetry and the Heroic Voice,* the first comprehensive study of the poet, was published by the University Press of Kentucky in 1987. It gave me great satisfaction to have Ms. Brooks inscribe my copy, "Thanks for pulling me into History." Three years later, the same press published my *Heroism in the New Black Poetry,* which won a 1991 American Book Award. That book ends with a poem appropriate to cite here. It expresses my perspective on and commitment to the poets I've written about. Their importance is no longer questioned. I like to think that to some modest extent, my work has made a difference.

For Black Poets Who Think of Leadership
D.H. Melhem

By song
through preacher
political
through field of hands and hearts
raising like wheat
the swords that are ploughshares
and the faces
that Malcolm and Martin saw
that Malcolm and Martin touched
with the colored strands
of their final vision

Black poets:
you enact the deep heroic line

Reading and Writing: The "Ever-Fixed" Compass Towards the North Star, Freedom
Lynnette C. Velasco

Wonder As I Wander, autobiographical, immortal words from an immortal soul, Langston Hughes. He walked humbly, listening, observing. He walked among both princes and sheep. Through his pen that never missed the bull's-eye, I found his quest infectious. His words invited me on a journey that I could neither deny nor resist. I, too, would join the ranks of scribes who want nothing more than to make their living writing poems and stories. I felt this calling somewhat divine yet laced with impending poverty. But, the magic, beauty, endurance, pride that was and is the black experience has led to a rewarding career journey and I have managed to pay the bills. Whether major or minor impact, I resolved that reading and writing about the never ending trials and tribulations of black folks would in some way along the long road of life get me closer to the North Star, towards freedom.

Black literature for black children and young adults written by black authors is my hue and cry. Reading opens doors, unlocks portals, spirits my imagination and fuels me with an empowering history of endurance and triumph. Writing is my way of paying homage to those authors who allowed me passage on the "underground railways." This passage is paved with conviction, commitment and dedicated bonding in an ironclad link to empower others on our "shared journey." Writing has healed wounds, quieted confusion, and provided sanctuary. Writing is my ever fixed compass, inching always toward the North Star. My choice to write for children and to advocate for Black literature for Black children and young adults written by Black authors stems from the fact that the literary experience nurtures potential. Potential is spirit and spirit in young people is fragile. It must be nourished and fortified with positive and reflective imagery so as not to be extinguished.

Many of our young people face daily challenges and incredible odds just facing the dawn of a new morning. Reading and writing is about hope, endurance, and victory. As a young reader, one of the many books that left a profound impact on me was Gordon Parks' autobiography, *A Choice of Weapons*. He overcame extraordinary odds to achieve brilliance in all of his creative endeavors. He states, "I choose my camera as a weapon against all the things I dislike about America—poverty, racism, discrimination." Like Parks, I have identified a weapon. My pen is my sword against injustice. The pen is my spark of knowledge pointing the way towards the North Star.

The literary experience should be a carefully guided one. Our young people cannot make this journey on their own. Family literacy must be a household staple. It is the only way our young can be guided through the many difficult twists and turns in this lifelong experience.

Though sometimes difficult to find, there are treasure chests overflowing with great books for our children. Parents, educators, librarians, guardians, and folks who are interested in positive growth and development of our young folks must get actively and progressively involved in order to instill the value and love of reading and writing in our young. We must become explorers enlisting/ drafting our young into our ranks, guiding them on a "shared journey," our compass ever fixed towards the North Star.

We must lay claim to and acclaim our black classics, particularly those works that are designed to reclaim, uplift, and empower our young. Newberry Medal Winner (2000), *Bud Not Buddy* by Christopher Paul Curtis is a captivating tale of a ten year old, Bud Caldwell, who is in search of his father. The tale is set against the backdrop of 1930s Depression-Era Michigan. The instinct and ingenuity for survival exhibited by Bud is sheer genius. Coretta Scott King Honor Book and National Book Award Finalist, *Monster,* by Walter Dean Myers is a uniquely, documented, fictional account of 16 year old, Steve Harmon, who abruptly arrives at the crossroads of life finding himself on trial for murder. This up close and personal story is boldly portrayed through the medium of screenplay and journal entries. *Death of Innocence: The Story of the Hate Crime that Changed America,* details the historical account of the murder of Emmett Till in 1955. This story of a fourteen year old boy from Chicago brutally murdered in Mississippi is a must read. The injustice of institutionalized racism and the century's old shame of America are exposed through the unforgiving pain of his mother's words, recollections and fact finding of author Mamie Till Mobley and co-author Christopher Benson. *47* by Walter Mosley and *Day of Tears* by Julius Lester are historically based accounts of systematic dehumanization that bred the culture that claimed Emmett Till as its victim. Mosley employs speculative fantasy, historical fiction and Lester combines historical fiction with a format of pure dialogue to tell harsh, graphic tales of men and women who although stripped of their dignity and deemed less than human, endured, discovered courage, reclaimed their dignity and rebuilt their self esteem. These brave heroes and sheroes, our earliest freedom fighters, successfully traveled the "shared journey" and followed the North Star all the way to freedom.

An intimate look into the life of Zora Neal Hurston in *Speak, So You Can Speak Again* by Lucy Anne Hurston celebrates her undeniable legacy in the annals of the Black literary movement in America. Zora Neal Hurston was somewhat of a maverick, a significant African American feminist who rejected the orderly middle class life of home-maker made her own independent way in the unpredictable world of the creative. Despite setbacks, she maintained her independence with few regrets. Jaira Placide's, *Fresh Girl,* a fictional portrayal of frustration, alienation, depression experienced by a fourteen year old immigrant, Haitian girl, is a classic yet unfortunate instance of modern day art imitating life. However, Placide brings her heroine to self-redemption and courage.

I cannot overlook today's cutting edge authors, Coretta Scott King Award honorees, Rita Garcia Williams and Sharon G. Flake. Daily our children are bombarded with negative imagery and false idols commonly adorned with what is termed, "bling." In their respective works, these authors dispel false illusions fed daily to our young. In *No Laughter Here,* Williams exposes the atrocity of female genital mutilation. On many levels, this is a coming of age book for young adults; however, her most significant message may be that it is emotionally crippling to remain silent in the face of injustice and that no matter what the consequence, one must find the courage of conviction to speak out against injustice. In *Bang,* Flake tackles the proliferation of violence, degradation and death that has become all too commonplace in black family life. Yet despite tragedy, she upholds the redemptive, enduring, healing and reconstructive legacy of Black family life.

We endure and we triumph. I applaud *Chicken Soup for the*

African American Soul: Celebrating Our Culture One Story at a Time, edited by Jack Canfield, Mark Victor Hansen, Lisa Nichols and Tom Joyner. It is a hearty potpourri of affirmation. We celebrate because we are survivors, conquerors, and our course is still ever fixed on a "shared journey" towards the North Star, all the way to freedom.

Read, write, read, write and then re-read and re-write, read to one another, read with one another and read to yourself. Reading and Writing are the Keys to Knowledge and Knowledge is the Key to the Door of the North Star and Freedom.

POEM TO A YOUNG BLACK MIND
Allyson Horton

come now born
beautiful ones
be intrigued
to know learn
acquire truths
modify myths
discover your
authentic value
against an un/authentic landscape
come now born
beautiful ones
open a book
of reliable source
& encounter who u
supremely are...

MALCOLM WAS MY MENTOR
Jamel Shabazz

One of the greatest turning points in my life came right after I read the *Autobiography of Malcolm X*. The year was 1976, and I was a Man/Child in search of knowledge. During that same year, the great Alex Haley shared his personal family history in the television Series, *Roots*.

Roots is the story of the African Holocaust, from the shores of Africa, to the plantations of the United States. Millions of Americans both Black and White tuned in daily to try and understand the pain and affliction of slavery.

For me, it started a sincere desire to learn as much as I could about the struggles of Black people both here and abroad. This is when I decided to read the *Autobiography of Malcolm X*, by Alex Haley. Upon opening the first page, I could not put the book down.

I was moved by the suffering that young Malcolm and his family endured living in Nebraska, during the early 1900's. I learned about family and survival. In Malcolm X's family, I saw a strong conscious father, who followed the teachings of Marcus Garvey, and who would later lose his life at the hands of White racists, for his beliefs.

As I diligently moved through each chapter, I was growing wiser with every paragraph. The turning point for me came after Malcolm X was incarcerated and received the life-giving teachings of the Honorable Elijah Muhammad. Mr. Muhammad became a father image to Malcolm, creating in him an unquenchable thirst for knowledge.

Turn The Page and You Don't Stop!

I studied how Malcolm X transformed himself from a petty thief to a studious, uncompromising fisher of men. Through Malcolm's example I developed a love for the dictionary, and for the power of words, and their meanings.

Malcolm X enabled me to have a better understanding of the struggle of people of color, both here and abroad. Prior to reading this book, I had little or no knowledge of President Nkrumah of Ghana, Sekou Toure of Guinea, Nelson Mandela of South Africa, and Ho Chi Minh of Vietnam, to name a few important world leaders.

In spite of having only an eight grade education, Malcolm X could debate university scholars with ease. Malcolm X's spirit will always live within me, and through his wisdom I have grown to be a Man committed to the struggle and purpose.

Recently, I retired from the New York City Correction Department where I had worked for 20 years [1983-2003] as a Corrections Officer. My duty assignment was Riker's Island, located in the Bronx, New York. Riker's Island is one of the largest prisons in the United States, with a yearly capacity of over 130,000, and a staff of 10,000 officers. The facility where I worked was the Adolescent Reception and Detention Center, better known as The Notorious C-74. This institution houses Pre-trial Detainees from 16 to 20 years of age.

I will never forget, my very first day at Riker's. I was a "New Jack"right out of the Academy, and despite my street and military experience, nothing could have prepared me for this environment.

I was walking past the receiving area for arriving and departing inmates when I came upon a holding cell that was jammed with Black and Brown detainees; they were packed in like sardines.

There were over 200 inmates in a cell designed for only 50. The only thought that ran through my mind was the horrible conditions on the slave ships.

Saddened by this sight, I realized that I had a duty to reach out and try to redirect the lives of some of these young men. I reflected on Malcolm X and his experience in prison, which allowed me to understand that every detainee had the potential to change if given the right opportunity.

To further help me understand prison culture, I read the book, *The Prison Letters of George Jackson*. Comrade George, as he was called, was sentenced to one year to life for an alleged armed robbery of a gas station for $ 71.00. He was eighteen, at the time.

While incarcerated at the maximum security Soledad Prison in California, George Jackson educated himself about the Black experience both here in America and in the Third World. Books and newspapers became a way for George to gain a greater degree of knowledge.

George Jackson, viewed as dangerous by prison officials, was placed in solitary confinement where he continued to educate and discipline himself. While in solitary he wrote two books: *Blood In My Eye and Soledad Brothers*. Both books became best sellers. George Jackson was killed by prison staff for reasons that are still not clear. He was 26 at the time of his death.

Both Malcolm X and George Jackson were guides for me. It's ironic that their books, helped to shape my foundation, and that I would become a Corrections Officer, working in a system that they both detested.

TURN THE PAGE AND YOU DON'T STOP!

I never wanted to be a tool of oppression. While working in the system, I devoted my time and energy towards helping inmates and fellow officers alike. Every chance I got, I passed on books to those who had a desire to change. I gave The *Autobiography of Malcolm X*, and *The Prison Letters, of George Jackson* to many young men in hopes that they would read them and make a change.

To help cope with this daily misery, on my days off I would take to the streets of Brooklyn with my camera and document the lives of the people in the community.

Photography become a way for me to unwind, and communicate to the youth in the streets about life and making the right choices. I always made it clear, where I worked and that I wanted the very best for them. These experiences, made me feel that I was part of the solution, and that I could make a difference.

One of my greatest joys is seeing men who have fallen victim to incarceration, change their lives around and begin giving back to the community.

Jamel Shabazz

BETWEEN THE LINES:
READING INTO THE SO-CALLED 'RAP WARS'
A short work of fiction, based on actual events
Ivory Achebe Toldson, Ph.D.

*Preface: Reading fills the void that exists between the lines you hear
and the things you see. The most dangerous thinking errors
occur when you believe anything, without reading something.*

BS World News

"*Who shot Sunni Sundiata?* is the question that's baffling the criminal justice system and the music industry alike. I'm Mike Lathers, here with BS World News, reporting live from Shriner's Memorial Hospital in St. Louis, Missouri. In a few minutes, Sunni Sundiata's expected to be released from I.C.U. He was shot last night as he was leaving his album release party.

"Right now I'm standing here among hundreds of fans who've come to show there support for the rap superstar after he made what doctors consider to be a miraculous recovery from head trauma. Let's get a few comments from fans while we wait.

"You ma'am, state your name and why you came here today."

"My name's Shanika Taylor, and I'm here becuz Sunni Sundiata is my-baby-daddy. And I love him so much. I LOVE YOU SUNNI!!!!"

"How about you sir, state your name and your reasons for coming here today."

"Yo... My name's Hak, and I'm a guerrilla! I wuz born in the struggle and I'mma die in the struggle! And I just wanna tell Sunni that the guerrillas in St. Lou gonna hold 'em down. We know that snitch Ammo wuz behind this, but St. Lou is Sunni Land, dig? Ammo, if you even think about showin' up in Da Lou we gonna..."

"Thank you Hak... I think that's all the details we need...

"I think I see Sunni now!

"Sunni?

"Sunni!!!"

The unsteady camera focuses in on Sunni, as he walks away from the hospital exit with his large entourage. Mike Lathers fights desperately through the cheering fans and competing reporters to get an interview with Sunni. Sunni walks tall, wearing baggy blue jeans, combat boots, and a black t-shirt with the words, 'guerilla warfare' printed diagonally across the front. He makes no attempt to conceal the bandage covering the bullet wound in the back of his shiny bald head.

"Sunni!!!" Mike Lathers calls out again.

With his shoulders squared and his red eyes piercing, Sunni halts his bodyguards and faces the cameras and microphones.

"Mr. Sundiata," Mike Lathers proceeds, "Many of your fans believe the rapper, Ammo, is responsible for shooting you. What're your feelings about that?"

"No feelings at all."

"I understand. But, are you afraid that hostilities between Ammo fans and your fans will increase the Black-on-Black violence already plaguing the Black Community?"

"With all due respect, Mr. Lathers, I don't think you or your viewers really care about the Black Community. If you did, you'd care less about who shot me, and more about whose shooting these black kids struggling to maintain in drug-infested communities. Besides, we never called your civil war White-on-White violence, so don't call my civil war Black-on-Black violence.

"Good day Mr. Lathers," Sunni concludes, signals to his crew, and walks away.

MVT (Music Video Television)

"Hey hey, this is Danena Dallas reporting live from MVT, bringing the heat from the streets. And ladieeeez, start fanning now because it's getting HOT! I'm standing next to one of the finest brothas in the rap game today... AMMO!

"Hiiiiiiii Ammooooo," Danena crooned.

"Whuz Happenin' Lil DD?"

"It's all about you Ammo! Your new single, "Pink Diamond", has been blazin' the charts, and your sophomore release, "Gold Rush", hits record stores tomorrow! First, tell us about this single... exactly what is a pink diamond?"

"Humph, check it... Figuratively speaking, a pink diamond is a sexy lady's hot spot, ya-know?"

[Lady fans screaming]

"OK ladies, you heard him!

"And speaking of diamonds? What's this I hear about a pink diamond blinging in yo teeth? Whassup with that, playboy?"

"Datz real," Ammo says, and gives an all-teeth smile for a close-up of the pink diamond stud chiseled in his tooth.

"That's HOT... Where'd you get a pink diamond? How much did it cost?"

"I copped it from a little Dutchman in South Africa. He let it go fa 'bout a hundred G's."

"One hundred thousand dollars!?! Must be nice!"

"OK, last question... You know a sistah gotta satisfy the rumor mill. The word on the streets is that you set Sunni up to get shot. What's the real deal, Fam? Set the record straight for the hatas."

"I can't fade it. Sunni probably shot himself as a publicity stunt. You know his CD drop tomorrow."

"So what's tha deal with the beef? Can two playas get along??"

"I ain't got no beef. Truth is, Sunni just wanna be on the same stage with me. He cooked up this beef 'cause I'm on top. And now he got these kids calling themselves guerillas.

"This is a message to tha kids: A guerilla ain't nothin' but a broke and angry loser. If ya wanna be mad just fa tha hell of it, and end up dead or in jail like Sunni's pappy, then follow up behind Sunni Sundiata. But it's too much money out here to be 'bout dat bull. Sheeezzz... while Sunni tryin' to build an army, I'm tryin' to build bank. So kids, don't be Sunni and don't be Ammo. Be you!

"And dat's all I gotz to say."

"And you heard it first on MVT. This is Sweet Danena Dallas, signing off. Cop that Gold Rush tomorrow! It's HOT!!!"

BS World News–Breaking News

"Mike Lathers here outside of the Ambassador Theatre in Sunni Sundiata's birth town of Yonkers, NY, where the saga continues between Sunni Sundiata and Ammo. Only hours after Ammo's live interview on MVT, he was assaulted in this theatre after his own concert.

"Here's what we have so far... About an hour ago, two men disguised as security guards ushered Ammo off stage, pulled him into

95

a utility closet, and beat him with a blunt object. They then removed his trademark pink diamond studded tooth. We were also told that the FBI is building a task force to investigate the latest upsurge of 'Rap Wars.'

"What's more, the assailants left behind a chilling letter that reads:

> *Ammo, We heard your interview on MVT and wanted to clear up a few misstatements. First, Sunni Sundiata doesn't make guerrillas. Greedy imperialists and ignorant sellouts like you make guerrillas. You might have the world fooled, but we know you're nothing but a two-faced snitch. How dare you floss a $100,000-pink diamond you bought from a Dutchman in South Africa? Do you know how many Black South Africans perished in diamond mines under Dutch colonial rule? This is now officially declared a conflict diamond and we're returning it to our revolutionary brothers in South Africa – Brothers in our worldwide network who share our struggle to reverse the global impact of centuries of oppression; not industry tricks like you. FREE KOFI SUNDIATA!*
>
> *The next day at work at the federal penitentiary...*

I proceed with my prison rounds stressing, *How am I gonna explain this rap war to Sunni Sundiata's father, Kofi Sundiata?*

When I reached the narrow window of Kofi Sundiata's cell in solitary confinement, he approached the window, eager to hear what I had learned about his son.

Without stalling I explained, "Someone shot your son in the head night before last, but he's OK now. Word on the streets is that this other rapper named Ammo set him up to get shot, but no one knows for sure. Then last night, Ammo was attacked at his own concert. He's still in the hospital now."

"SUNNI WAS SHOT??? Oh my God!!!" Kofi stressed.

"Yeah, I know. And right after Ammo was attacked, the reporter read a letter from the attackers that ended with the phrase, 'Free Kofi Sundiata.' But no other coverage mentioned the letter. And today, the reporter who read the letter was fired—some guy named Mike Lathers."

"Mike Lathers? That's the journalist who wrote a book about me."

"Really? Was it a good book?" I asked, "I mean... did it portray you in a favorable light?"

"There were a few minor omissions, but overall, I was pleased with it."

"OK, I'm about to ask a stupid question, so just bear with me. But, why did a white journalist write a book about you?"

"Because at the time, no black journalist wanted to. But enough about him, did you hear anything else about Sunni?"

"Well, there's also a family suing him; claiming their son shot a police officer under the influence of his song, 'Pig Roaster'."

"That's absurd!" Kofi exclaimed.

"Yeah, that's a little far out there. But a lot of people believe it. People are saying all kinda stuff about Sunni. A naval officer on TV last night said Sunni's probably getting funding from terrorists. And this professor from Christian Wright Academy said you're probably orchestrating the Rap War. He accused you of being an 'anti-Christian, anti-American communist'."

"Fools!" Kofi lambasted, "They're all fools! Before they put me in this hole, I was the one telling Sunni not to engage in this war with Ammo. I was teaching him to respect women and not to pollute his mind with drugs.

"They are the ones instigating this rap war! Planting informants who introduce narcotics into his crew!! Enticing him with loose women!!! Henpecking and instigating differences between Sunni and Ammo!!!! And they won't stop until this illusion they so insidiously call a 'rap war' ends with both Sunni and Ammo dead or in jail!!!!!

"And who ultimately wins this so called rap war? Not Sunni, not Ammo, not me or you, but them... They win."

"Who's *they*?" I asked.

Kofi took a deep breath to calm himself, then explained, "They are people in this society who want to maintain the status quo. Just like Mike Lathers explained in his book."

"So, this book... would help me understand who 'they' are?" I asked.

"It might also help you understand who you are," Kofi replied.

"I don't get it," I puzzled.

A tear fell from Kofi's eye as he continued to plead, "The media's portraying Sunni as a psychopath, but he's not. He is a loving man with a verbal gift from God. If you check Sunni's criminal record, you'll find he's completely crime free. Sunni's only crime is his last name."

"But Mr. Sundiata, with all due respect, aren't some of Sunni's lyrics a little violent?"

"Well, so is U.S. foreign policy. Censorship and democracy is another debate. Right now, all I'm saying is that Sunni hasn't broken the law, and shouldn't be denied his father's guidance.

"Listen, I know it's very difficult to understand what's going on right now. My son and I have been victims of character assassination, and it's probably hard for you to trust us. But I'm not asking you to trust me. Trust your gut."

Later that evening, I went to my neighborhood bookstore and found Mike Lather's book. It covered COINTELPRO—The United States' secret war against Black Nationalism. The book explained that in the 1970s, Kofi Sundiata was uprooted from his movement, and replaced with a drug dealing government informant named Lu. Lu ran the streets until the 1980s, when the government flipped the script and turned the War on Black Nationalism into the War on Drugs. The War on Drugs rang on throughout the 1990s, but soon revolutionary Hip Hop promised a new resistance in the new millennium. So before 'gangstaz' became guerillas, Rap Wars were contrived, using the same East Coast vs. West Coast tactics that pummeled the Black Panther Party in the 1970s. Biggie Smalls became Eldridge Cleaver, Tupac Shakur became Huey Newton, and White-on-Black violence became a puppet show called Black-on-Black violence. But the only way to see the strings is to read between the lines.

I now know that we need to honor our martyrs, understand our history, enthrone a vision for our future, and most importantly, avoid duplicity by reading!

TURN THE PAGE AND YOU DON'T STOP!

Suggested readings:

Churchill, W. & VanderWall, J. (1990). *The COINTELPRO Papers: Documents from the FBI's Secret War Against Dissent in the United States.* South End Press.

Dyson, M. (1996). *Between God and Gangsta Rap: Bearing Witness to Black Culture.* New York: Oxford University Press.

Books:
The Key to Our Past, Present, and Future
Latoya Wolfe

Throughout my early childhood, I received "good grades" and praise from my teachers for high test scores, but was I undisciplined, and rarely studied anything. Though I was attentive in school, when I got home, it was all about doubled-dutch and my Atari 2600. Back when I was young, I spent most of my time outside playing rope, hand games, and running to candy store; there were no books in the street, and few inside of my house. My mother, faced with the challenge of raising a son and a daughter in the Robert Taylor Homes, was content with having children who went to school, stayed out of trouble, and were respectful. Later though, I realized what I was missing.

Though I was a good kid, and I enjoyed my youth, college slapped me in the face with an angry hand. Since I was the first person in my family to attend a four-year university, and I had moved onto campus, my family was unaware of the support that I needed. I was dropped off at school and left with no emotional or financial support from my family. I scraped to afford my books, I did not know how to study, and I was far behind everyone in class because they had attended schools with rigorous academics.

My grades were barely average in all subjects except for English, where I excelled. I decided to explore English as a major, and I hit the jackpot. Most of the early English requirements were composed of research papers, essays, and creative writing. I loved to write, but I was not fascinated with the idea of reading since it was associated with the dry British Literature and History from high school. Since I didn't grow up reading books I was ignorant to the fact that there was literature out there that I would enjoy.

After workshopping my very first short story, an English teacher's critique included a suggestion to read Toni Cade Bambara's *Gorilla My Love*. I ran to the library to find the book. I discovered that it was a short-story collection, and as I read the stories, I was amazed at what this Black woman was writing about. "The Lesson," one of the stories from the book, reminded me of kids that I grew up with. I began to seek more books by people who looked like me, spoke like, and ate the same foods that I grew up eating. I enrolled in a Black Women Writers class and there, I discovered Toni Morisson's *The Bluest Eye*, Ann Petry's *The Street*, and *Incidents in the Life of a Slave Girl*, a disturbing tale by Harriet Jacobs. These women were born and raised in a different time, but I was astonished at how relevant their stories were to my present-day life.

Writing lead me to reading, and today I read in order to study what other writers have done with story, but also to learn about my culture, my history, and my future. It's amazing what a book can do. I often-times reflect on my childhood and I wonder about all of the time I spent playing, and what would be different if I traded in some of that play time for reading.

Books are More Than Just Words
Traycee Lynn

Before 1996, I was an "off and on" reader. During those times, different people and experiences would motivate my reading, but nothing seemed to keep me inspired to read more regularly. My father was the first person to encourage me to read. He had a checkered presence in my life. Sometimes he was there, often he was not. Although his visits were random, he always brought me a book as a gift. This was odd because I was a child who preferred toys. I did not complain, though, because I was always happy to see him. Instead, I latched on to those books, stacked them neatly, and declared war with siblings and friends if any one of my books were ever missing or damaged. The books represented my father. They took his place in his absence, so I wanted to read books mostly because he gave them to me. After a while, his visits slowed and so did my reading.

As I grew into my teens, my mother inadvertently motivated my reading by leaving a novel on the kitchen table. It was *Mama* by Terry McMillian. I remember being drawn to it because it was the first book that I noticed with Black people on the cover. I would get home before her and I, eventually, finished the book before she did. We began talking about it. I guess it was our unofficial book club. The next thing I knew, she was bringing home more books by McMillan to share with me. I read most of McMillian's novels but was not inspired to explore other books in the house that were mostly written by white authors such as Stephen King and Jackie Collins. After *Disappearing Acts,* I stopped reading again.

TURN THE PAGE AND YOU DON'T STOP!

The greatest experience that helped me to understand the importance of reading occurred around my senior year in high school when I was getting ready for college. I was ranked in a top percentile of my graduating class and was considered to be a "high achiever."

However, at my college orientation I learned that I was not the high achiever I'd been labeled in high school. College placement, test results showed that I was not on the college level in math or reading. Apparently, the college preparation I had received at my inner city high school was nowhere near the college preparation that my white suburban peers had enjoyed. (They came from schools that had more money, resources, and more highly qualified teachers.) Therefore, in order to bring my skills up to the college level, I had to take remedial classes that did not count towards my degree, but were necessary if I wanted a degree. I spent my freshman year and part of my sophomore year catching up to my peers who were more likely to graduate on time.

I remember feeling bamboozled by my high school, and in that moment I began to take my education into my own hands. I realized that if I had been reading more regularly and widely, I might have been more informed about what it meant to be on the "college level." I might not have been distracted by those colorful, ego-feeding labels like "high achiever"—labels that only mattered at my high school, but had no real value once all students across the country were merged together in one university.

After this revelation of my own ignorance, I developed a regular habit of reading. I read a wide variety of newspapers, magazines, books, flyers—everything. I did not limit myself to catchy titles, headlines, or subjects of immediate interest, so in addition to Black lives, I read about the lives of other races, science, religion, business, relationships, parenting and so on. The more I read, the more I knew that it would be impossible to know everything, but having a general foundation on common things was definitely beneficial to my intellectual advancement.

I consider these experiences from grade school to college as beacons that helped guide me toward my path as an arts media agency. In 2002, I was 25 years old and I started my own newspaper in Philadelphia, called *Writer Blocks*. At that time, I did not know how serious of a step I had casually taken. I did not know the power that I was claiming as a young, Black female in America by starting my own media force. I was also unaware of all of the influential Black writers of the early 1800's like Samuel Cornish and John Russworm who were responsible for the first Black newspaper in the United States called *Freedom's Journal* (1827-1829), and Frederick Douglass' *North Star* (1847-1860), Willis Hodges *Ram's Horn* (1847) and so many others who also started their own newspapers. All I knew was there seemed to be a lack of media outlets for young Black arts and culture community in Philadelphia, and as a fellow artist, I shared the same pulse and wanted to do something about it.

I learned that in order to take on any type of entrepreneurship, it is necessary to be well-read in the subject matter and knowledgeable about the history and the changes taking place in the industry. So, in addition to the history of the black newspapers, I began to read a variety of newspapers and books to study various writing styles, examine the way people thought, and to expand my own knowledge bank. I noticed that reading and writing had a direct connection. The more

I read, the more my writing style, vocabulary, business sense, and public speaking improved. All of this was beneficial in the progress of taking a two-paged newsletter of 100 copies distributed locally to twelve-paged newspaper of 5,000 to 10,000 copies distributed throughout the tri-state region. So by the third year, there was a strong buzz in the city, I formed relationships with contributing writers throughout the tri-state, and the newspaper began to pay for itself.

Overall, I realized that reading impacts my life on so many levels, probably more than I will ever know. I believe that the development of the publication is a reflection of my own personal development through reading. If I am stunted in thinking and limited in perception, it will reflect in the content of the newspaper and anything that I write, whether it be an article, song lyrics, or poetry. Therefore, I'm always looking to read and expand my horizons realizing that education does not begin nor end with a diploma or degree, and that cultivation of the mind is a lifetime process enhanced by a regular habit of reading.

READING MAKES CENT$
Hadassah Hickman

L ike many of today's youth, I began reading because it was forced upon me by the school system as a requirement. It was also a mandatory part of my upbringing. Reading later became an important part of my growth and development process.

The summer I turned twelve, signaled a change from the previous eight summers I'd spent participating in my local library book-a-thon and provided a break from the one thing I dreaded more than anything, reading. That summer I began working in my parents' furniture store and quickly grasped the entrepreneurial concepts of "buy low, sell high" and "always fill a need." I enjoyed the sense of freedom making my own money gave me much more than competing in the book-a-thon. The following summers I continued to work for my parents and in my senior year stumbled across my father's book, *Think and Grow Rich: A Black Choice* by Dennis Kimbro.

Reading *Think and Grow Rich* unlocked my imagination, empowered me to form a vision for the things I wanted in life, and most importantly, helped me rediscover the power of reading. I began spending hours in my father's library out of sheer desire to become informed on the subjects that piqued my interest and allowed me to cultivate my dreams of entrepreneurship.

That was ten years ago and a lot has changed in our society that makes it more feasible than ever for youths to start businesses. Significant technological changes, an influx of publishing dedicated to small business and entrepreneurship, numerous organizations and web sites all make it easier for youths to explore business ownership. According to a study conducted by Youth Intelligence, 25 percent of youth ages 13 to 24 would consider themselves successful if they owned their own business. Young people are not only dreaming about starting businesses more today than ever before, they are taking control of their futures and starting companies younger and faster.

Technological changes in the last decade have made it simpler, faster and less expensive to access information needed to start a business and create a business plan. Websites like www.youthstartups.com cater to youth and provide a plethora of ideas, success stories and articles. Youths conducting research can also search multiple library databases at www.libraryspot.com. Regardless of age or socioeconomic background, today's youth should spend a little time on the internet and in libraries reading, researching and writing their business plan.

Youth entrepreneurship programs are popping up in schools and communities across the country and on the Internet making it easier to network with other youths considering entrepreneurship. Additionally, a number of organizations offer summer camps for teens interested in entrepreneurship. *Black Enterprise Youthpreneur* www.blackenterprise.com and National Foundation for Teaching Entrepreneurship (NFTE) offers summer camps in New York dedicated to teaching 13-18 year olds the fundamentals and importance of entrepreneurship. Owning your own business is a lonely venture, but sites like www.YoungEntrepreneur.com connect business owners of all ages and create a virtual support system for those that lack the resources at home. Disney's Hot Shot online game www.disney.go.com/hotshot allows typical 9-12 year olds to simulate life as a business owner. Players can find or borrow money to open businesses like a skateboard factory, pet spa or comic shop.

The majority of businesses that youths start require very little capital. For those that require additional capital, young entrepreneurs should consider performing chores, small fundraising activities, or borrowing from friends and family to start their business. Magazine founder, Kenya James had a dream of starting a magazine dedicated to African-American girls. She did not have the required capital to start her company so she decided to sell home-baked goods. Kenya saved her profits and founded *BlackGirl* magazine at the age of 13. It is not unheard of for youths to spend $150.00 on a pair of gym shoes. That same $150.00 can be used to build a website on www.register.com, order business cards at www.vistaprint.com, set up a toll free number at www.voice-plus.com, legally setup your business as a sole proprietorship in your local county, and meet your first potential client for a cup of joe at your local coffee shop. Did I mention you'll have change for lunch the next day?

Reading coupled with entrepreneurship is one of the greatest tools our youth can seize today to take control of their future. Let's face it; we do not live in a society with equal access to education and social and economic resources. But, our society does offer today's youth the opportunity to improve their lives through entrepreneurship. Consider Farrah Gray, author of *Reallionaire* who was born into poverty and raised in a single family home. By the age of 14 he'd grown from public assistance to self-made millionaire through the sale of his food company, Farr-Out Foods. Twenty or thirty years ago when America's richest entrepreneurs like Bill Gates and Paul Allen of Microsoft or Michael Dell of Dell Computers began their businesses as teens it was almost unheard of. Today, it is not rare to read headlines about youth entrepreneurs like Cameron Johnson who began an

Internet empire at 9 that now generates over a million dollars in revenue or Michael Furdyk, a successful young entrepreneur, who sold his business, MyDesktop.com, for $1 million when he was 16 years old!

Although, today's youth have given up the lemonade stands for office space, websites, Fortune 500 clients like Verizon, BET, or McDonald's; entrepreneurial principles remain the same. Buy low and sell high, fill a need, or create a product or service with a distinct competive advantage. Although this is not a recipe for success, Camilla Amber White, founder of Jam-N-Yams', would disagree. "Some might say that you're too young. But you should do all that you can to achieve your goals. You are never too old or too young to own and operate a business," says White, who began her catering company at age 8 and now offers more than 40 cakes and pies.

As an entrepreneur, now I read to stay informed and make decisions on market changes that affect my business. I'm a big believer in youth entrepreneurship and the rewards that come from starting young and dreaming big. I'm a believer because I live it and you can too!

Additional Resources:
Books

What Color Is Your Piggy Bank?: Entrepreneurial Ideas for Self-Starting Kids by Adelia Cellini Linecker

The Young Entrepreneur's Guide to Starting and Running a Business by Steve Mariotti

Websites

www.youngbiz.com: Offers summer camps, articles and links to games for preteens & teens.

www.nfte.com: Through entrepreneurship education, NFTE, which is also referred to as Network for Teaching Entrepreneurship, helps young people from low-income communities build skills and unlock their entrepreneurial creativity

www.entre-ed.org: For teachers, instructors, program developers and others who help students of all ages find their own entrepreneurial opportunities.

www.e-magnify.com/envision: e-magnify.com, the website of Seton Hill University's National Education Center for Women in Business hosts this informative site to foster the development of entrepreneurial skills among the next generation of workers.

www.sba.gov: U.S. Small Business Administrations official website that provides a wealth of information on starting, financing, and marketing a business.

www.kidscamps.com: Provides list of summer camps including business camps for youth.

www.mysummercamps.com: Provides list of summer camps including business camps for youth.

www.celcee.edu: Easy-to-use site provides abstracts on entrepreneurial research and education.

TELLING THE STORIES
Wade Hudson

When I was growing up in the segregated South in the 1950s and 1960s, books were an important part of my world. I read everything biographies, novels, essays. Books allowed me to look outside my small, provincial town in Louisiana. Although I felt protected and cared for by my family and my community (which was a difficult challenge in segregated Louisiana), I knew a different world awaited me. This world, though filled with its own challenges, was where I would find my place. Books helped me to understand that place.

Books took me places I could never go physically. In books I met people who were famous and those who lived ordinary lives. Books allowed me to travel into the past and take adventurous sojourns into the future. They helped me better understand the world in which I lived. They liberated me. They helped me feel good about myself. They let me know that I was important even when others around me told me that I was not. Books became some of my best friends.

My world of books was not all rosy. Not many of the books I read featured African Americans as characters. Those that did often portrayed us as pathetic creatures with very little to offer society. But I was able to cut my way through the vines and the undergrowth that sometimes hid the humanity. It was there, where the humanity was laid bare, that I could identify with the characters and the stories and find myself. Humanity is the place where we all connect, and where we all find our being. The vines and the undergrowth are what we use to cover it up, to hide it.

The more books I read, the more I realized that our stories, our history, had to be told. I was not aware of Richard Wright, Ralph Ellison, Langston Hughes, or Gwendolyn Brooks. I had never heard of the Harlem Renaissance or Paul Laurence Dunbar. But I had

this burning desire to one day tell our stories. I wanted to give people the opportunity to see the glory and majesty of our experience as African Americans as well as the pain and the anguish. So I set out to tell our stories. And along the way I learned that many other blacks had sat down pen in hand, to tell our stories, too. Many had done so decades before my humble attempts.

My life's journey has taken many twists and turns. But books and the desire to tell our stories have always been constant, whether with poems, plays, essays, or songs.

In 1988, my wife, Cheryl, and I started a children's publishing company, Just Us Books. We recognized the need not only to tell our stories but to publish them as well to affirm our history and culture for children. We also knew how important it was for children, particularly black youngsters, to see children who look like them in the books they read.

We located our company in the New York metropolitan area, home of the book publishing industry, where many established writers and artists live and thrive. New York is noted for its racial and ethnic diversity and its many forums that allow for a wide range of voices to be heard. Cultural, art, and music institutions seem to be everywhere. But as we made plans to launch our company, these important factors were not paramount. Rather, we thought about *Freedom's Journal,* the first black newspaper, and its first editorial written by Samuel Cornish and John Russwurm in 1827. "We wish to plead our own case," it read. "Too long has the public been deceived by misrepresentations, in things which concern us dearly."

We thought about the words of Langston Hughes, a giant of the Harlem Renaissance. In an essay entitled "The Negro Artist and the Racial Mountain," Harlem's adopted son wrote: "We younger Negro artists who create now intend to express our individual dark-skinned selves without fear or shame...We build our temples for tomorrow, strong as we know how, and we stand on top of the mountain, free within ourselves." We thought about the Schomburg Center for Research in Black Culture, and we knew we could utilize its great collection of books, photographs, manuscripts, films, and recordings. We thought about many other important events, people, and places in African-American history that have New York City connections. We knew we were in the right place to launch our company.

We celebrated our fifteenth year in publishing in 2003. Just as *Freedom's Journal,* the Harlem Renaissance, and the Schomburg Center have made an impact on society, we know Just Us Books has, too.

A Passion for Publishing
Felicia Pride

When I tell people I have a master's degree in writing and publishing, I always get some sort of puzzled look. I can see the questions whirling around in their heads. Why? Publishing? What does she mean? Is she mistaken?

Why? publishing?

The writing part makes sense, but publishing?

I can't blame them. For one, I could have easily followed the money-making career track of some of my friends. An MBA (masters in business administration) or law degree would have probably secured me a higher paying job and crazy fringe benefits (hey, now that I work in publishing, I get more free books than I would have ever imagined.)

Sometime during college though, while studying for an undergraduate degree in marketing, I was hit with a serious jones, an intense love affair with the written word. Trust me, I tried resisting. How could I find a career dealing with words? I didn't really consider myself a writer, but I was a reader, loved books, and wanted to find a way to be involved with the creation of them. But I really didn't know how. At that time, I didn't realize there was an entire industry dedicated to producing books. The disconnect between publishing and writing is fairly common. It's funny how one rarely thinks about how a book is made. To many people these bound pages just magically appear in bookstores.

But we all need to think more about this process. Publishing is the way by which our stories are documented and distributed. It is the eternal mate of writing. Without publishing, there would be no books. An easy conclusion, yes, but consider for a minute its implications.

Without publishing, there would be no books.

So I took a chance. I followed my passion and fascination for books and enrolled in Emerson College's graduate program in writing and publishing to immerse myself in the business that brings words to the masses. Ironically enough, I found out that the people involved in bringing words to the masses did not reflect the diversity of the masses. Publishing is an industry that severely lacks people of color. My graduate program was no different. As I looked around at my classmates, my future career peers, who were, for the most part, white, I knew that I had a mission before me.

It hit home even further when I interned at a well-respected, progressive publishing house. Call it a life-changing epiphany. I was sitting in an editorial meeting while the publisher, VP of marketing, publicity director, and acquisitions editors, discussed what books would and would not get published. I looked around the room and noticed not one person of color present. Not one person of color offering their two cents on what books deserved to be published. Not one person of color explaining why a certain book or author is important. Not one person of color combing the headlines and suggesting important topics that justify attention in a book. This, I thought to myself, was the epitome of cultural gate-keeping.

This is around the time that I started BackList, www.thebacklist.net, a website dedicated to keeping books in style, specifically, texts of interest to people of color. I saw a need for a venue that would engage in both a literary and publishing discussion. What began as a newsletter to fewer than one hundred people morphed into a well-respected website with thousands of visitors and content hard to find anywhere else. Through BackList, I've had the opportunity to interview authors that I admire, help authors promote their work, and truly embark upon a career in literary activism.

But this passion didn't stop there. Upon graduation from Emerson, I landed a job at a major publisher in New York City. Talk about a dream come true! Of course there was a lot of hard work involved and sacrifices made. Did I mention that publishing jobs won't make you a millionaire? Yet, now that I'm living and working in the publishing capital of the United States, I've been able to expand my passion into organizing literary events around New York, I've gotten additional freelance and consulting work for writers and have received numerous invitations to give my opinion about the literary world.

All of this because I like to read. Who would have thought it would have transformed into a meaningful and important career that I love?

Walter Mosley once said in an interview, "The people who go into publishing are also going to be the people who change the world. And it's a world that needs changing."

I couldn't have said it better myself. I guess you can say I'm up for enacting a little change, one book at a time.

THE DC WRITERSCORPS WAY
Kenneth Carroll

L et me warn you before I start; this idea of strengthening literacy
by teaching literature is not popular among traditional non-profit funders. In an education system now obsessed with standardized
testing, creative writing workshops for youth are seen as a waste of
valuable test-prep time. So if you're working with a non-profit that
must seek foundation support, you'll probably want to avoid the DC
WritersCorps way of strengthening literacy. However, if you want to
give youth a reason to read and write other than the platitude of "you
need to get a job and/or go to college," DC WritersCorps has a
proven, but simple, method of inspiring young people through literature.

I'm executive director of DC WritersCorps, a program started ten
years ago as a collaboration between the National Endowment for the
Arts and President Clinton's AmeriCorps program. The idea was to
find ways to get working writers involved in improving their communities. Our mission is to use the literary, media, and performance arts
to reorient student's attitudes toward reading and writing. Our goal is
to get them to see reading and writing as a joy and a lifelong tool for
success in and beyond the classroom.

Writer Toni Cade Bambara once wrote that the job of writers in
an oppressed society is to make revolution irresistible. I would add
that the function of literature in any society is to make reading
irresistible. Literature, whether it be David's Psalms or Amiri Baraka's
poetry or August Wilson's plays, or Ernest Gaines short stories, or Toni
Morrison's novels, is the sweet reward one gets for having learned

how to read. The ability to read contracts or academic text is a necessary function-the grunt work of being able to decipher words and syntax. Literature is the exaltation of reading, the bling of comprehension.

Most of the over 100 writers who've taught at DC WritersCorps over the past decade, became writers and avid readers because one day, at some time, we opened a book of literature and found ourselves in the story. Our heart rate and breathing increased. We were moved to tears, laughter, rage, or all three. We wanted to replicate the emotions produced in us by the skill of the author. We wanted to be as musical and as relevant as Amiri Baraka praising John Coltrane while condemning the Ku Klux Klan. We wanted to be as sensual as Sonia Sanchez is as she explored the possibilities of clean and honest love while she explicated the dankness of sexual exploitation. And so we took pen to paper and tried to create our own worlds and our guides were the great Canon of world literature.

In DC WritersCorps, we teach creative writing workshops to about 500 students a year in 11 DC middle/junior high schools. We do not dictate the bibliography of our instructors or the methods they use. Instead we say to them, find the broad spectrum of art that excited you and come up with innovative ways to use that work and the memory of that excitement to get students to write about every thing from their neighborhood to their mother's addiction. Or we say bring in Thelonious Monk and get the immigrant student from El Salvador who misses his abuelita in San Salvador to try and reproduce the spectrum of sounds and emotions produced by Monk's music. Or we say bring in the mural by Jacob Lawrence and ask your sixth grade class, who pronounce the "w" in sword and the "l" in Salmon, to retell the story told in the earth tones of Lawrence's brush.

Turn The Page And You Don't Stop!

We do not participate in the grading systems in the classrooms, nor do we tie our workshops directly to the school's curriculum. This is done for two reasons; we do not want students to associate our workshops with grades, and two; in Washington, DC we have a school system where statistically half of the students will fail to get a diploma. We are in no hurry to tie our wagon to a dying horse. Our instructors do, however, work closely with the classroom teachers and may connect individual lesson plans with the teacher's curriculum goals, but they aren't required by DC WritersCorps to do that.

This is not to suggest that our program is all Birkenstock sandals, locked hair, and peace signs. We have outside evaluations that substantiate the efficacy of our non-traditional methods. We have outcomes that our writing instructors are required to produce through their workshops. We first of all want students to write. We provide journals for each student and work with them to fill up as many pages as our budget can stand. We encourage them to write through in-school writing exercises and through after-school assignments designed to keep the pen on their pages long after class. Some out-of-class assignments (the term homework is verboten in our workshops) might be for the student to record their dreams for a week, to simply inventory, without comments, the contents of their room, to write a letter to deceased relative. We want students to write raps, poetry, short stories, and notes to themselves, rambling stream-of-consciousness love letters, goofy stuff, and neighborhood slang. But they must write, especially if they want to remain in our after-school writing clubs.

We require our instructors to set up opportunities for students to be publicly celebrated for their writing skills. This is important. In a society that is more likely to reward youth of color for their athletic and entertainment prowess, we want our students to be celebrated for their intellectual and creative skills in producing meaningful writing. We provide our students with as many opportunities to read in front of diverse audiences as we can. We've done monthly readings at community centers, bookstores, museums, and libraries. Hell one year I got some fifth grade students a paid gig reading poetry at a Kwanzaa celebration at the local lottery board. It is a moment in their lives to be acknowledged for their skill and courage. They got a chance to understand the efficacy of writing and the profundity of their own voices.

We also want students to read literature-lots of it. Our writers duplicate thousands of individual poems, excerpts from fiction and non-fiction, and occasionally, as our budget allows, we purchase and give away books to our students. Our goal is to have students take these great pieces of literature away from the class with them. The mother of one of our students talks about how her daughter reads to her the literature she receives in our workshop as she prepares dinner. We want students to read Haki Madhubuti as they rock Kanye West in their iPods on the Metro. We want students to start a library in their living rooms, stacking the poetry of Laini Mataka on a shelf near the TV in their home that regularly advocates for their marginalization. We encourage our students to start their own literary libraries. The goal is helped by our partnership with businesses like Borders Books and our current partner Karibu Books.

In addition we bring living writers to our classrooms and we bring our students to living writers. We want our students to meet, commiserate, and talk junk to, fawn over, and be amazed at meeting a great writer. I grew up in Washington, DC and did not meet a living writer until I was 26 years old. Writers and students must be bought together so that the reality of the possibility of writing as a vocation or an ad vocation is made real. They must understand that books are not created by magic, but by the talents and skills of somebody with blood coursing through their veins and demons to exorcise—just like them. We want writers to come and tell their stories of tragedy and triumph. We want students to know that writing can save you, or at least keep you whole enough to save yourself. And we want them to know that writing can make a difference, can cause someone to want to know more.

A few years ago Nikki Giovanni did a benefit reading for DC WritersCorps, before the event she met with young writers from our program and signed copies of her book, which we purchased for them. As I was driving one of the students home after the event, she sat nearly catatonic, hugging her signed book to her bosom, her eyes glazed over with excitement. When I asked if she was happy to have a signed book by Nikki Giovanni, she said, "yes, but I'm more happy that she talked to me, as if I were a writer just like her." Then the student paused and said to me, "I wonder if she knows she's Nikki Giovanni?" It is that wonder we want them to experience, to have award winning writers like Quincy Troupe, Jeffery McDaniel, Van Jordan and others who have met with our students, speak to them as if the ten line poem they wrote had as much meaning as any poem they've read.

We want students to understand the essentials of poetry, its basic elements and techniques and we want them to be able to break a poem down, to grapple with its meaning, apparent and subliminal. We want them to understand the precision of word choice, the importance of brevity, the gravity of images. And lastly we want them to use literature to help them interpret and reinterpret the world. Unlike the poet Archibald Mcleish, we want them to understand that a poem, like their lives, can "mean" and "be" at the same time. We want them to understand as Chinua Achebe reminds us, that the poet must stand with the people. And we want them to understand that, as Baraka explained about his own writing life, "My writing came out of me without too much formal grunting and extrapolation of the dry." We want them to understand that this is possible. As Williams Carlos Williams was fond of saying, "if it ain't a joy, it ain't a poem." We want them to know that poetry can be a joy even as it speaks to us of pain. We want them to understand that as Patricia Smith tells us, they can resurrect dead loved ones through the simple, but powerful act of reading and writing.

Gaston Neal, a great poet and activist, who was, in many ways a guide as we struggled in the early years of DC WritersCorps to connect writers with community, often told our writers during his training workshops, "In our arrogance, we miss 99 percent of all the poetry in the world." Gaston's words were a warning for our writing instructors; many of whom had MFAs and were armed with the ability to formally grunt and produce extrapolated dry on command. It was a warning to not just teach poetry but to find it. To not just give students short stories to read but to discover stories in their faces. To find dramatic tension in the students simple, yet courageous act of making it to school despite the drama going on at home. June Jordan admonishes us in a quote, "you will never teach a child a new language by ridiculing the language they currently speak." I remind our writers that when we go into the communities of DC to teach creative writing to youth, we are not going there to teach them to fly, instead our job is to remind them, they already have wings. That's the DC WritersCorps way.

"I WANT TO BE A WRITER," SHE SAID.
Opal Moore

"**B**ut I don't like to read. I want to write poetry," she said, "but I hate reading poetry."

I can't remember the first time a student said this to me. I remember being startled. I remember pausing and looking at her, looking carefully—I thought I'd misunderstood. She looked back, summoning a defiance that said, "yeah, I said it. So what?" I remember thinking, in that silent standoff moment: I want to be a singer, but I hate music. I want to be a dancer, but I don't like dancing. I want to be a piano player, but I hate piano music. I want to be a mother, but I hate kids.

I remember feeling something that I could not find words to describe. So I just decided to remember the feeling. To her I said, well, in this writing workshop, we read. A lot.

When I was a kid, I always wanted to be an adult. My mother would always say, "enjoy your childhood, you'll be an adult soon enough." This was odd coming from my mother because her own childhood, from what she'd related to us kids, had been no stroll in the park. But, though my own childhood was, as Nikki Giovanni would say, "quite happy," I had had enough of childhood by the time I was nine or ten.

Of course I understood that I had no job and no way of earning a living, but that to me was one of the flaws of childhood—the child's necessary dependence, the inability to achieve any kind of independence. It was true that adults had all the worries of finances and "putting food on the table", but they were well compensated for that, weren't they? They could be seen AND heard. They had rights–the rights I'd learned about in school. They had a Bill of Rights. They had freedom of speech, freedom of the press, freedom of movement. They had uncensored access to their own minds. No adult was ever *shushed*. I'd never heard any adult say to another, *don't speak unless you are spoken to*. I equated adulthood with wholeness.

I was not a cute child—I did not have wavy hair or big, liquid eyes, or the cherubic cheeks and poultry lips of the knee-bounced child. To make matters worse, I was a quiet child, so adults did not "take to" me. I later learned that quiet children make adults nervous. Quiet children seem to be thinking, something considered inappropriate to childhood. Suspicious. A quiet child was either scheming or possibly retarded. In fact, I *was* thinking. I was thinking that children were not whole—we were incomplete people. I wanted to be an adult, not because I was anxious to have sex (didn't know what it was) or a job. I wanted to be complete.

I found that in books. My first ideas of independence and personal agency were fostered by the actions of characters that I found in stories. And stories, for the most part, were captured in books. It did not matter to me whether I read the Bible or a cookbook. I was entranced by the way that words, so slight, so flat, so silent, lifted off of the page to become a vision in my mind. These stories filled in the blanks of my black life, my life unbracketed by the life stories of my parents or grandparents. Those generations, through some silent agreement, had determined that the stories of their struggle and hardship were stories not to be passed on. Their silences were, I think, intended to be our guarantee of happiness. How could they know it would leave us unhinged as new doors.

I learned in school about the mass black migrations, but I did not know the story of how my own recent ancestors had come out of the South and settled in Chicago. I did know how Moses led the Israelites out of Egypt, and about their wandering in the wilderness. I did not know how my grandfather, who had probably not completed grade school, acquired two properties in Chicago, an independent taxi cab business, and founded a church. Instead, I knew how Booker walked from West Virginia to Hampton and gave himself a middle name (Taliaferro) and last name (Washington) and built a college. While there were great lessons in mental toughness and determination and ingenuity that I could have learned from the people who raised me, they were not a storytelling people. In books, I discovered other versions of the stories that my own people had buried. I found the stories that the Tradition, The People, had determined to preserve. These stories were secondhand, but they were still mine. And so, it was through books that I understood how real defiance is often silent, founded on preserving principles and driven by personal courage, which is mostly determination.

These people that I encountered in books were willing to give me their stories so that I could figure out my own way of meeting the challenges I would surely face. They put their lives up for scrutiny in a way that my personal exemplars—the people who taught me important cultural values and philosophies, fed my body and my confidence, sent me to school—could not bring themselves to do.

I know that this discovery of important, grounding stories of historical black people struggling to impose their will upon an unwelcoming world provided the passion behind the rage of my generation, the generation that insisted on bringing African American literature and culture studies to America's classrooms—it was in books that we discovered that we were not a new invention, not new doors without hinges, but something very old, very connected and connecting, very profound. We needed those stories. Not to build our racial ego, but to build our inner selves. To build the society that we said we wanted to live in. These were not stories of martyrs, but men and women who wanted to rewrite the human covenant.

"I want to be a writer, but I don't like to read," she said.

In my role as a teacher, I get to hear a lot about what young people think of reading and writing. Some tell me that reading and writing is for eggheads. "I'm a do-er," they say, separating thinking from doing. Increasingly we are suffering as a country from this kind of segregation of intelligence from action. Others tell me that reading is "too hard;" it's too hard to translate language into purpose. Writing is "too hard," translating thought into organized written words. I think of reading and writing as the first tools we are given to discover ourselves—a discovery that is more important than that of the Spanish explorers or astronauts collecting rocks from the moon. Understanding ourselves is the first step to doing almost anything—it's the first step to purpose. Even something as simple as baking a cake requires a level of commitment, planning and preparation. But tell that to the government officials who read the five-part reportage in the *New Orlean's Times Picayune* in 2002 detailing the impending disaster that so surprised everyone when it occurred three years later. If young people tell me that they don't like to read, or that writing is a waste of time, it's got to be, in part, because they see no regular connection between writing, reading, and doing something really important. Neither do the "adults" running their country.

But then, I was an odd child. As I said, I always wanted to be an adult. Who can sympathize with such an eccentric perspective in a time when childhood lingers way past post adolescence into middle age? But I was wrong in my first assumption—that becoming an adult (i.e., of legal age) made one complete. It's harder than that. From Thomas Paine, pamphleting the populace on the complexities of liberty in an effort to help this nation to grow up, to the writing act of the Constitution, to Frederick Douglass pressing that document into public service, to Zora Neale Hurston who stitched the black folk voice to the literary, to Dudley Randall who built the backbone of a literary revolution with the creation of Broadside Press, and all the other thinkers and writers in between and beyond—through them I have been made to see the connection between reading (signs and documents), writing and world shaping.

A young writer wants to write. She does not want to read. To whom does she write? Does she write for herself alone? Okay, She loves being a door without a hinge. Very well. But from what timber will she hang herself? Does she dream of a world of doors with no house to which she might serve as an entryway?

Notes on Contributors

Cory Anderson, a trained journalist, works for the Winthrop Rockefeller Foundation as a senior program officer in Little Rock, AR. Cory is married to an educator, Dr. Phyllis Nichols-Anderson, and has four children.

Melrita Bonner is a retired librarian with the Central Arkansas Library System and volunteers as a reader for various blind and vision impaired services in Little Rock, Arkansas, where she lives with her husband.

Traycee Lynn (Tracey Lynn Bryant) is the founder of Writer Blocks newspaper and the Society for Urban Literary Arts, a non-profit organization in Philadelphia. She is also a poet, songwriter and radio talk-show host on WURD 900AM and WPEB 88.1FM in Philadelphia.

Kenneth Carroll, founder and executive director DC WritersCorp teaches writing workshops for teens at Montgomery County Community College and for the Writers Center. A native Washingtonian is married and the proud father of a daughter and two sons.

Reverend Marrice Coverson is pastor of the Church of the Spirit, founder and president Institute for Positive Living and Executive Director Open Book Program.

Frank Frazier is largely a self-taught artist whose work has been featured in books, films and television and movies like, *Waiting to Exhale, Coming to America, Frank's Place,* and *Bustin' Loose.* Exhibitions of his art include shows at the African American museum, Hempstead, New York; Armour J. Blackburn Gallery, Howard University, Washington, D.C.; Martin Luther King Jr. Library, Dallas; and the Brooklyn Museum. He resides in Dallas with this wife Judy.

Patrice Gaines is author of the autobiographical *Laughing In The Dark, From Colored Girl to Woman of Color—a journey from prison to Power* and the inspirational *Moments of Grace: Meeting the Challenge to Change.* She lives outside Charlotte, N.C., where she is co-founder of The Brown Angel Center

Sandra Y. Govan is a professor of English at the University of North Carolina at Charlotte. She has published in *Black American Literature Forum, The Langston Hughes Review, Erotique Noire* and *Langston Hughes: The Man His Art and His Continuing Influence.* She contributed the "Afterword" to the reissue of Octavia Butler's *Wild Seed.* Govan is a member of the Wintergreen Women Writers Collective.

Hadassah Hickman is President of Sitar Capital Group, a full-service business development firm. Hadassah is a passionate advocate for small business and has facilitated youth entrepreneurship, financial literacy, and business development seminars and workshops in the U.S. and Africa.

Victor Hill BA, MA and JD, has served as Eastern Arkansas Circuit Judge since January 1, 2001. Victor is the devoted father of daughter, Imani.

Allyson Horton is a native of Indianapolis, IN. appeared on Showtime at the Apollo where her winning performance gained her national recognition. Allyson has opened for noted poet Nikki Giovanni and inspirational speaker - Iyanla Vanzant.

Wade Hudson is the president and CEO of Just Us Books, Inc. an independent publishing company he founded with his wife, Cheryl Willis Hudson. Mr. Hudson has written more than 20 books for children and young adults. Mr. Hudson lives in New Jersey with his family.

Andrew Jackson has been executive director of Queens Borough Public Library's Langston Hughes Community Library and Cultural Center for the past 25 years. His latest projects include a book, pending publication, entitled *Queens Notes: Facts about the Forgotten Borough, Queens, New York*.

Parneshia Jones works in publishing for Northwestern University Press. Her awards include the Gwendolyn Brooks Poetry Award and the Margaret Walker Short Story Award. Parneshia lives in Evanston, IL.

Janis F. Kearney, a writer, lecturer and oral historian, recently published *Cotton Field of Dreams: A Memoir*. In 2004, she founded Writing our World Press, a small Chicago-based publishing company. She is currently a Visiting Fellow at DePaul University's Humanities Center.

Haki R. Madhubuti is an award-winning poet, publisher, editor and educator. His latest release is *YellowBlack: The First Twenty-One Years Of A Poet's Life: A Memoir* (2005). He is the founder and publisher of Third World Press (1967). He is the Distinguished University Professor and professor of English, Chicago State University.

Dr. Julianne Malveaux, an economist, author and commentator, is the President of Bennett College and President and CEO of Last Word Productions, Inc. Her most recent book *The Paradox of Loyalty: An African American Response to the War on Terrorism* (Third World Press 2003).

D. H. Melhem, Ph.D., CUNY, M.A., CCNY, B.A. NYU, wrote *Gwendolyn Brooks: Poetry and the Heroic Voice,* the first comprehensive study of the poet. Her Heroism in the New Black Poetry, a National Endowment for the Humanities Fellowship study, won an American Book Award.

David C. Miller, M.E. is the co-founder and Chief Visionary Officer of the Urban Leadership Institute, LLC and author of several books including *Dare To Be King: What If the Prince Lives a Survival Workbook for African American Males?* (2003 & 2004). David lives in Baltimore, MD.

E. Ethelbert Miller is a literary activist and board chair of the Institute for Policy Studies (IPS), a progressive think tank located in Washington, D.C. His latest book is a second memoir, *The 5th Inning* published by Busboys and Poets Press, 2009. Site: www.eethelbertmiller.com.

Opal Moore is author of *Lot's Daughters*. Her fiction and poetry have appeared in various publications. Moore is a Fulbright Scholar, a Dupont Scholar and recipient of the Bellagio and Mellon Fellowships. Her suite of poems, "The Children of Middle Passage" is forthcoming in a "picture book" for adults with artist, Arturo Lindsay.

Useni Eugene Perkins is author of several books of poems, plays and non-fiction including his latest *Harvesting New Generations*. In addition, he is the President of the Association for the Positive Development of Black Youth and has been recognized as one of the pioneers of the Rites of Passage movement.

Felicia Pride is the founder of BackList (www.thebacklist.net), an organization dedicated to harnessing the power of words to uplift communities. A writer, teacher, and lecturer, she's also the author of several books including *The Message: 100 Life Lessons from Hip-Hop's Greatest Songs* and the YA novel, *Patterson Heights*.

Jamel Shabazz is the author of *A Time Before Crack* (2005), *Back in the Day* (2001) and *The Last Sunday in June* (2003). Shabazz's photography has been exhibited at the numerous galleries around the world. Shabazz lives in Long Island, New York.

Irene Smalls, BA, MBA, Award-winning Author/Storyteller/Historian educates. Her presentations includes core components of literacy instruction for students K-5 using a variety of instructional approaches and for older students she discusses the publishing, the writing, the job of being a writer and risk taking.

Dr. Ivory Achebe Toldson is an author, psychologist, Howard University professor, and clinical consultant for the Manhood Training Village. He is the author of *Black Sheep: When the American Dream becomes a Black Man's Nightmare.* Dr. Toldson currently lives with his wife in the DC Metropolitan area.

Lynnette C. Velasco, poet and author of the children's book, *Zinzi: A Child's Journey to Self Fulfillment, Giving and Caring.* Lynnette is a consultant to the Center for Black Literature at Medgar Evers College of the City University of New York and a contributor to Black Issues Book Review. She is the President of Black Americans in Publishing.

Latoya Wolfe is the recipient of the Zora Neale Hurston/Bessie Head Fiction Award, the Union League Civic and Arts Foundation Short Story Award, and the Betty Shifflett/John Schultz Short Story Competition. She lives in Chicago.

Randall Horton is the author of The Definition of Place (Main Street Rag, 2006) and co-editor of Fingernails Across the Chalkboard Poetry and Prose on HIV/AIDs from the Black Diaspora (Third World Press, 2007). He has a MFA from Chicago State University and is a PhD from SUNY Albany. Randall is also a Cave Canem fellow.

Afterword

Turn the Page and You Don't Stop is an impressive collection of essays, commentaries, stories and poems that celebrate the importance of reading as an indispensable tool and resource to enhance a person's cognitive development and knowledge of life. Indeed, even those skeptics who do not appreciate the power and compassion of the written word will be impressed by the writings in this literary gem. These writings are crafted by a wide and diverse range of successful writers who share with us how reading has contributed to their own careers and achievements. For example, Janis F. Kearney, the author of the best selling autobiography, *Cotton Field of Dreams: A Memoir,* and President William Jefferson Clinton's personal diarist, reveals how her share-cropper father and God-fearing mother made personal sacrifices to ensure that all of their children received a quality education. University professor, poet, memoirist, and critic, Dr. Sandra Y. Govan, tells with humor and passion the story of how she was driven to become a reader as she matched wits with a despotic grade school teacher. Dr. Julianne Malveaux, nationally recognized economist, syndicated columnist, and author, fondly recalls how her early passion for reading proved to be more than an enjoyable pastime.

These are just a few among the many often poignant stories told by contributors to this book who acknowledge reading as being the spring-board for their personal and professional development. It is important to note that these writers come from various professions, but all trace their life's work back to an important encounter with the written word.

Each in her or his own field or literary genre provides us with personal testimony to the inherent value of reading. Wade Hudson and Kenneth Carroll have created programs and institutions designed to share their passion for reading with others. Hudson is the founder of Just Us Books, a publishing company specializing in books for children; Carroll has served as the executive director for the DC Writers Corps, founded ten years ago. Another contributor, Marrice Coverson, founded the Open Book Program that brings Chicago Public School students together with nationally known authors.

This book will surely be a valuable tool for educators, youth advocates and social practitioners to utilize as an inspirational text for young people who may or may not consider themselves "readers." It may prove a useful resource—some of the contributors identify important programs and opportunities for the curious. It may also serve as an encouragement to the "closet reader," someone who loves books but may fear being labeled as "uncool."

Reading is the fountainhead of academic achievement. We must all make a concerted effort to instill in our young people a desire to read and work to create environments that encourages reading.

Finally, Patrick Oliver, a long-time advocate of promoting reading programs for youth, should be commended for conceiving and editing this important book. One can readily discern that he treasures the values inherent in reading and also wants our youth to develop a passion for the written word.

—Useni Eugene Perkins

Second Edition
Printed in the United States of America

Special thanks to Opal Moore
Front and back cover paintings by Frank Frazier
Cover design and book layout and design by Denise Borel of Borel Graphics
Inside photography by Jamel Shabazz

ISBN: 0-9779499-0-7 (alk. paper).

Permissions to reprint

"Our Lessons in Life..." appears in *Cotton Field of Dreams: A Memoir* copyright 2005 by Janis Kearney, reprinted by permission of Writing Our World Press, Chicago, IL.

"Free Public Libraries: Democracy's Real Test", appears in *Tough Notes: A Healing Call for Creating Exceptional Black Men* copyright 2002 by Haki R. Madhubuti, reprinted by permission Third World Press, Inc., Chicago, IL.

"For Black Poets Who Think of Leadership" appears in *Heroism in the New Black Poetry: Introduction and Interviews* copyright 1990 by Dr. D.H. Melhem, reprinted by permission University Press of Kentucky, Lexington, KY

"Omar, Books and Me", appears in *How We Sleep on the Nights We Don't Make Love* copyright 2004 by E. Ethelbert Miller, reprinted by permission, Curbstone Press

"My Nephew Erik", This story is part of Opal Moore introduction of Gwendolyn Brooks at Radford University in March, 1991.

A portion of the proceeds from the sale will benefit the *Say it Loud!* public programs. Since 1997 *Say it Loud!* Readers and Writers has provided an opportunity for children, youth ages and adults to participate in activities and events designed to enhance their appreciation for literature as a tool for personal, educational and career development.

Inquiries email info@speakloudly.com or visit our website www.speakloudly.com

TURN THE
PAGE
AND YOU
DON'T
STOP!

Sharing Successful
Chapters in Our Lives
with Youth

Second Edition

Edited by
Patrick M. Oliver

Foreword by Randall Horton

Say It Loud! Readers and Writers Series

TURN THE PAGE AND YOU DON'T STOP!